BIOLOGICAL ASPECTS OF BEHAVIOUR

Longman Essential Psychology
Series editor: Andrew M. Colman

Other titles in this series:

Abnormal Psychology
Arnold A. Lazarus and Andrew M. Colman

Applications of Psychology
Andrew M. Colman

Cognitive Psychology
Christopher C. French and Andrew M. Colman

Controversies in Psychology
Andrew M. Colman

Developmental Psychology
Peter E. Bryant and Andrew M. Colman

Emotion and Motivation
Brian Parkinson and Andrew M. Colman

Individual Differences and Personality
Sarah E. Hampson and Andrew M. Colman

Learning and Skills
Nicholas J. Mackintosh and Andrew M. Colman

Psychological Research Methods and Statistics
Andrew M. Colman

Sensation and Perception
Richard L. Gregory and Andrew M. Colman

Social Psychology
Michael Argyle and Andrew M. Colman

BIOLOGICAL ASPECTS OF BEHAVIOUR

EDITED BY

Daniel Kimble
and
Andrew M. Colman

LONGMAN
London and New York

Longman Group Limited
Longman House, Burnt Mill
Harlow, Essex CM20 2JE, England
and Associated Companies throughout the world.

*Published in the United States of America
by Longman Publishing, New York*

© 1994 Routledge
This edition © 1995 Longman Group Limited
Compilation © 1995 Andrew Colman

This edition first published 1995

ISBN 0 582 27812 0 PPR

British Library Cataloguing-in-Publication Data
A catalogue record for this book is available from the British Library.

Library of Congress Cataloging-in-Publication Data
A catalogue record for this book is available from the Library of Congress.

Typeset by 25 in 10/12pt Times
Printed and bound by Bookcraft (Bath) Ltd

CONTENTS

NOTES ON EDITORS AND CONTRIBUTORS

ANDREW M. COLMAN is Reader in Psychology at the University of Leicester, having previously taught at Rhodes and Cape Town Universities in South Africa. He is the founder and former editor of the journal *Current Psychology* and Chief Examiner for the British Psychological Society's Qualifying Examination. His books include *Facts, Fallacies and Frauds in Psychology* (1987), *What is Psychology? The Inside Story* (2nd edn, 1988), and *Game Theory and its Applications in the Social and Biological Sciences* (2nd edn, 1995).

LEONARD W. HAMILTON received his doctorate in biopsychology from the University of Chicago and is now Professor of Psychology at Rutgers University in New Brunswick, New Jersey. He has published articles on the limbic system and behavioural inhibition and is co-author (with C. R. Timmons) of a textbook entitled *Principles of Behavioral Pharmacology: A Biopsychological Approach* (1990).

J. ALLAN HOBSON is a Professor of Psychiatry at Harvard Medical School and Director of the Laboratory of Neurophysiology, Massachusetts Mental Health Center. A prominent figure in modern brain science, his major research has been on the neurobiology of the sleeping brain. He has won the prestigious von Humboldt award of the Max Planck Society. He is the author of *The Dreaming Brain* (1988) and *Sleep* (1989).

DANIEL KIMBLE is Professor of Psychology and Neuroscience at the University of Oregon. He took his doctorate in psychology at the University of Michigan in 1961 and after a postdoctoral stay at Stanford University, California, joined the faculty at the University of Oregon in 1963. He was named a fellow in the American Association for the Advancement of Science in 1988. He has published numerous articles on the role of the hippocampus in behaviour and on the functional effects of brain grafts in mammals. He is the author of several texts in biological psychology, his most recent book being *Biological Psychology* (2nd edn, 1992).

C. P. KYRIACOU Charalambos Kyriacou is Reader in the Department of Genetics, University of Leicester. He began his career as a psychologist and obtained his doctorate in behaviour genetics at Sheffield University. After periods at Brandeis University, Massachusetts, and in the Psychology Department at Edinburgh University, he moved to Leicester in 1984. His current research interests are in the molecular genetic analysis of behaviour. He is the co-editor (with B. Holland) of *Genetics and Society* (1993).

JOHN LAZARUS took his PhD at the University of Wales and is currently at the Department of Psychology, University of Newcastle upon Tyne. His research interests are vigilance, anti-predator behaviour, sampling, sexual strategies, and parental care. In addition to his theoretical and experimental work, he has conducted fieldwork in Britain, Iceland, Australia, and Tanzania.

C. ROBIN TIMMONS received her masters degree in biopsychology and her doctorate in developmental psychology from Rutgers University, New Brunswick, New Jersey. She is now Associate Professor of Psychology at Drew University, Madison, New Jersey. She has published articles on the development of behavioural inhibition and memory in infants, and is co-author (with L. W. Hamilton) of a textbook entitled *Principles of Behavioral Pharmacology: A Biopsychological Approach* (1990).

SERIES EDITOR'S PREFACE

The *Longman Essential Psychology* series comprises twelve concise and inexpensive paperback volumes covering all of the major topics studied in undergraduate psychology degree courses. The series is intended chiefly for students of psychology and other subjects with psychology components, including medicine, nursing, sociology, social work, and education. Each volume contains five or six accessibly written chapters by acknowledged authorities in their fields, and each chapter includes a list of references and a small number of recommendations for further reading.

Most of the material was prepared originally for the Routledge *Companion Encyclopedia of Psychology* but with a view to later paperback subdivision – the contributors were asked to keep future textbook readers at the front of their minds. Additional material has been added for the paperback series: new co-editors have been recruited for nine of the volumes that deal with highly specialized topics, and each volume has a new introduction, a glossary of technical terms including a number of entries written specially for this edition, and a comprehensive new index.

I am grateful to my literary agents Sheila Watson and Amanda Little for clearing a path through difficult terrain towards the publication of this series, to Sarah Caro of Longman for her patient and efficient preparation of the series, to Brian Parkinson, David Stretch, and Susan Dye for useful advice and comments, and to Carolyn Preston for helping with the compilation of the glossaries.

ANDREW M. COLMAN

INTRODUCTION

Daniel Kimble
University of Oregon, USA

Andrew M. Colman
University of Leicester, England

Psychology is a dynamic and exciting field of study. One of the reasons for its appeal to many people is that it has intellectual links to several other disciplines, such as philosophy, psychiatry, sociology, and – the focus of the essays in this book – biology. Several areas of great relevance to the study of behaviour within the biological sciences are discussed in this book. There is a chapter on behavioural genetics; another on behavioural ecology and evolution; an essay on "the organ of behaviour", the brain; a chapter on basic states of the organism, such as sleep and dreaming; and a concluding essay on how drugs affect our brains and thus our behaviour (psychopharmacology).

As biological beings, we share a common heritage. We all began as a union of chromosomes from our parents, 23 pairs from each. On these chromosomes, composed of deoxyribonucleic acid (DNA), there are an estimated 100,000 genes, of which perhaps as many as 70,000 are expressed in the construction of the brain and nervous system. Thus, any fundamental understanding of our behaviour must consider the contribution that genetics has to offer. Modern genetics, which began with the insightful studies of an Austrian monk and amateur botanist called Gregor Mendel (1822–84), is now a scientific endeavour of dazzling new techniques and extremely rapid progress. For example, modern techniques of genetic engineering allow researchers to extract DNA molecules from cells, cut these molecules into precise pieces, recombine them with other DNA fragments, and insert this recombined DNA into host organism cells where they can control the production of proteins (see Bryan, 1995, for a full discussion of these techniques). Also, the combined efforts of geneticists around the world in the Human Genome Project are in the process of elucidating the entire DNA sequence for human beings (Bodmer, 1995). Psychologists, particularly those concerned with biological aspects of behaviour, need to be at least somewhat familiar with modern genetics.

In chapter 1, on heredity and behaviour genetics, C. P. Kyriacou discusses several basic ideas in the field of behavioural genetics. His chapter discusses research with both human and animal populations. The topics covered in human behavioural genetics include intelligence (as measured by IQ tests) and psychopathology (as manifested in schizophrenia). Three main methods are used in such research: twin, family, and adoption studies. For a further discussion of the ideas behind these methods, see Segal (1993). Perhaps most revealing are studies of correlations between identical (monozygotic or MZ) twins and fraternal (dizygotic or DZ) twins. For both kinds of twins, correlations of IQ scores are relatively high (.86 for MZ twins and .60 for DZ twins, on average). From these and other comparisons, Kyriacou concludes that roughly half the phenotypic variation in intelligence is due to genetic differences and about half to environmental influences. Similar analyses on MZ and DZ twins, in cases where one or both individuals have been diagnosed as schizophrenic, reveal a substantial genetic component to this disorder as well. Bipolar disorder, according to Kyriacou, also has a substantial genetic component. It is important to keep in mind that the existence of a genetic component does not mean that a characteristic is genetically determined, and the role of environmental events needs to be considered as well. For a more detailed review of the interplay of hereditary and environmental influences on behaviour, see Plomin (1994), and for a controversial interpretation focusing on intelligence, see Herrnstein and Murray (1994).

The power of modern behavioural genetics is clearly shown in Kyriacou's analysis of several different areas of research in animal behaviour genetics. Much of this research has been done with the fruit fly, *Drosophila melanogaster*, the stalwart of genetics for many years. In this organism, mutations in single genes can affect not only body colour but also visual behaviour, sexual behaviour, and locomotor activity. With animals, one can employ biochemical, physiological, and molecular techniques to add even further to the power of the method. Kyriacou predicts that molecular neurobiology will become the major life science in the next century.

In chapter 2, which is devoted to behavioural ecology and evolution, John Lazarus focuses on evolutionary aspects of human and animal behaviour. For Lazarus, behavioural ecology is "the branch of psychology whose aim is to understand behaviour in terms of a history of evolutionary adaptation". According to Darwin's theory of evolution by natural selection, the frequency of a gene in a population increases if it improves the *fitness* of the organisms that possess it (see, for example, the excellent account in Dawkins, 1986). Fitness, in turn, can be defined as lifetime reproductive success. While this idea may appear tautological (genes that improve fitness must increase in relative frequency, because the organisms that inherit these genes will produce more offspring and thus more genes), some behaviours that have evolved are not so readily explained. For example, how do we account for the alarm call of a bird that sees a predator? Surely this call attracts the attention of the predator to the bird raising the alarm, thus reducing the chances for that particular bird to survive and to pass on its genes. Lazarus discusses such altruistic behaviours, along with other seeming paradoxes (see Colman, 1995, ch. 11, for a discussion of these problems within the framework of game theory). Other areas he covers include social behaviours, aggressive behaviours, parental care, competition for mates, and mate choice.

Behaviour is produced by activity in the brain and nervous system, as are all our thoughts, dreams, and emotions; in short, all mental content. In chapter 3, "The Nervous System and the Brain" by Daniel Kimble, the organization and functional principles of these organs are discussed. The basic unit of the nervous system is the neuron. Neurons generate both electrical and chemical signals as they communicate with each other and with other cell types. Andrew Hodgkin and Alan Huxley worked out the basic nature of the electrical signal, or nerve impulse, in the 1950s and 1960s. Although there are many variations on the basic theme, the nerve impulse is initiated by an inrush of sodium ions to the inner surface of the neuronal cell membrane, and restoration of the original resting condition is achieved by an outrush of potassium ions from the interior of the neuron. These ion movements take place through specific ion channels in the cell membrane, channels which open and close as a function of the electrical potential across them. The nerve impulse serves to carry information from one region of a neuron to another. Other ions, particularly calcium and chloride, also play a role in the electrical activity of the neuron and participate in additional functions within the nervous system.

Neurons also secrete specific chemical substances, called neurotransmitters, that are responsible for carrying information from one neuron to another, and from neurons to muscle and gland cells. A number of such neurotransmitters are known, and drugs that interact with this process of *synaptic communication* form the basis for the field of psychopharmacology (which is dealt with in chapter 5 by Leonard W. Hamilton and C. Robin Timmons). Such chemical communication also makes use of a wide variety of ion channels to produce postsynaptic potentials, which differ from nerve impulses in several fundamental ways.

The functional neuroanatomy of the brain and nervous system is another major focus of chapter 3. Special emphasis is placed on the evolution of the forebrain, and in particular on the cerebral cortex. This portion of the mammalian brain is thought to be primarily responsible for the evolution of advanced skills such as language comprehension and production, abstract reasoning, and artistic creativity. One significant development in recent years is the growing evidence for the *modularity* of the primate brain, such that different cognitive processes appear to depend on specific neural circuitry. One clear example of this is the localization of much of the circuitry for language production in one cerebral hemisphere – usually, but not always, the left hemisphere. Modern techniques for imaging the human brain while it is performing meaningful cognitive tasks promise to usher in a new era for understanding its functions. As Kimble concludes, "prospects for understanding the functions of the human brain have never been brighter".

We spend a third of our lives asleep, and in recent years knowledge of sleep and dreaming has increased dramatically. J. Allan Hobson's chapter on sleep and dreaming (chapter 4) defines three basic behavioural states: waking, non-rapid eye movement sleep (NREM), and rapid eye movement sleep (REM). These states can be defined, according to Hobson, in terms of EEG records, source of input (internal or external), quality of thinking, and presence or absence of movements. The significance of REM sleep has been known since the early 1950s, when research by Aserinsky and Kleitman (1953) demonstrated the high degree of association between REM sleep and dreaming. In recent years, progress has been made in understanding the underlying cellular neurophysiology of sleep and dreaming; at the core of this research is the concept of a reciprocal interaction between two key neurotransmitter systems. These two systems, with critical circuits located in the pons and medulla, are the *cholinergic system* and the *aminergic system*. Hobson extends these concepts into a neurophysiological account of dreaming. Any such theory, he argues, must account for four basic aspects of dreaming: (1) that the brain is in a highly active state during dreaming; (2) that most of the sensory input from the outside world is blocked from access to the brain during REM sleep; (3) that motor movements are inhibited and blocked from overt expression during REM sleep; and (4) that there are rhythmic bursts of activity from the pons (called PGO waves). The chapter concludes with a consideration of the puzzling problem of the functions of sleep and dreaming. Research seems to support Shakespeare's idea that sleep "knits up the ravelled sleeve of care". Rats, deprived of sleep, cannot long survive; they lose such vital controls as thermoregulation and metabolic homeostasis. It appears that the immune system may also suffer with inadequate sleep. Functions for dreaming remain unknown. Hobson speculates on several possibilities, most of which involve information processing and storage that must occur during REM sleep.

The study of how drugs affect mood and behaviour is called psychopharmacology and chapter 5 by Leonard W. Hamilton and C. Robin Timmons concludes the book with a discussion of this topic. Psychoactive drugs are currently used in two basic ways: to alter mood states, and to treat various types of psychopathology, such as schizophrenia and chronic anxiety.

Included in the mood-altering drugs are stimulants such as dextroamphetamine, cocaine, nicotine, and caffeine. These drugs are used to produce psychomotor arousal, inhibit sleep and drowsiness, and, in children, to treat attention deficit disorder. The underlying cellular neurophysiology is different for each of these drugs, underscoring the idea that no simple or unified explanation for a category of drugs is likely to exist. What does seem to be true is that virtually all psychoactive drugs interact with one component or another of synaptic communication, as described in this chapter (for details on synaptic communication, see also Kimble's chapter on the brain and nervous system). Another class of mood-altering drugs is the depressants, exemplified by such compounds as morphine, heroin, and alcohol. As their name implies, these drugs are used both medicinally and recreationally to produce sedation, and for pain relief and anxiety reduction. Most of these drugs are thought to interact with one or another part of the GABA (gama-amino-butyric acid) receptor complex, which is found in the cell membrane of neurons throughout the nervous system.

Since the introduction of the use of chlorpromazine for schizophrenia in the 1950s, there has been a revolution in the treatment of the mentally ill. While it can be argued that drug therapy for such conditions as schizophrenia, depression, and anxiety can produce undesirable effects, it is clear that the introduction of drugs for mental illness has fundamentally changed how we view psychopathology and its treatment. Among the major classes of drugs used to treat psychological disorders are antipsychotics, such as chlorpromazine, and more recent drugs, such as clozapine. The leading theory concerning the primary mechanism of action in all such drugs is that they block receptors for the neurotransmitter dopamine; but serious difficulties still remain with this hypothesis. Antidepressants such as imipramine and fluoxetine appear to block the reuptake of aminergic neurotransmitters such as noradrenalin and serotonin, thus increasing the amount of these transmitters in the synaptic cleft. Anti-anxiety drugs such as alprazolam and buspirone are useful in many cases, although the primary mechanism of action may be different in these two drugs. Lithium salts are now the drug of choice for bipolar disorder. Here the mechanism of action is not known; but the efficacy of lithium for bipolar disorder is one of the success stories in psychopharmacology.

Although the use of drugs to treat mental disorders is certain to continue, and perhaps to expand, such drugs are not without side effects, and they do not work for all individuals. This is a challenge for future psychopharmacologists, as is the serious, and as yet unsolved, problem of addiction. This is not a new problem, as alcohol and drug abuse probably antedate written history, but these problems still cost the individual and society dearly. Understanding of drug and behaviour interactions will require an increased knowledge of the basic principles of synaptic transmission, in particular, and of brain function in general.

The chapters that follow should serve as a useful introduction to the basic problems and the hard-won information about biological aspects of behaviour. For readers who wish to pursue any of the topics in greater depth, suggestions for further reading are supplied at the end of each chapter. It is hard to imagine a more interesting or rewarding subject, or for that matter a more relevant one for the improvement of the human condition.

REFERENCES

Aserinsky, E., & Kleitman, N. (1953). Regularly occurring periods of eye motility and concomitant phenomena during sleep. *Science, 118*, 273–74.

Bodmer, W. F. (1995). *The book of man: The Human Genome Project and the quest to discover our genetic heritage*. New York: Scribner.

Bryan, J. (1995). *Genetic engineering*, New York: Thomson.

Colman, A. M. (1995). *Game theory and its applications in the social and biological sciences*. Oxford: Butterworth-Heinemann.

Dawkins, R. (1986). *The blind watchmaker*.Harlow: Longman.

Herrnstein, R. J., & Murray, C. (1994).*The bell curve: Intelligence and class structure in American life*. New York: Free Press.

Plomin, R. (1994). *Genetics and experience: The interplay between nature and nurture*. Beverly Hills, CA: Sage.

Segal, N. (1993). Twin, sibling, and adoption methods: Tests of evolutionary hypotheses. *American Psychologist, 48*, 943–56.

1

HEREDITY AND BEHAVIOUR GENETICS

C. P. Kyriacou

University of Leicester, England

The genetic analysis of behaviour has a long history, beginning with the twin studies conducted by Galton (1869) in the nineteenth century. In the 1920s, with the environmentalism of J. B. Watson dominating the intellectual atmosphere within psychology, a few islands of nativism were to be found, the most important being in the laboratories of E. Tolman and R. C. Tryon. In a two-generation artificial selection experiment, Tolman produced evidence that rat "intelligence", as measured by the number of errors made by rats trying to find their way around a maze, had a significant genetic component. Tryon extended and improved the procedure and produced his famous "maze-bright" and "maze-dull" lines within a few generations of selection (Tryon, 1940).

In the 1950s investigators began in earnest their attempts to get to grips with "behavioural genes". Margaret Bastock and Aubrey Manning studied the genetics of behaviour in the fruit fly *Drosophila*. They concentrated on the stereotyped "fixed-action-patterns" that make up the courtship interactions of the male and female. By investigating these instinctive behavioural "elements", they reasoned that the genetic substrate for behaviour would be more evident, compared to more complex motor programmes where learning might be involved. P. L. Broadhurst, at the Maudsley Hospital in London, also began selecting for "emotional" versus "non-emotional" rats in an open-field arena. Clearly there was a "psychological" perspective to this work, as the Maudsley reactive and non-reactive strains (as the two selected lines were called) could, at least at face value, provide an animal model for "neurotic" behaviour. Tolman, Tryon, and these British workers in the 1950s were truly pioneers, but converts to the cause of behaviour genetics were rather thin on the ground.

In this review, I shall attempt to assess the more significant developments in the area. A number of excellent textbooks exist to introduce the reader, including Plomin, Defries, and McClearn (1990) and Hay (1985). The latter part of the discussion that follows will draw heavily on molecular biology, which is becoming increasingly important in behaviour genetics.

NATURE AND NURTURE

Any behaviour requires movement, and motor structures such as muscles, glands, etc., are built by genes. Thus all behaviour has a strong genetic component. The interesting question is whether behavioural *differences* between individuals are due predominantly to genetic or to environmental factors, and what is the scale of their respective contributions. Let us consider the case of "identical" or monozygotic (MZ) twins. They have all their genes in common, but environmental influences mean that we can usually tell them apart quite easily, simply by looking at them. So even when there are no genetic differences, the environment can produce differences between two individual "clones". This example illustrates how the environment can mould differences in even genetically identical individuals. The obvious conclusion is that whatever behavioural or morphological character you examine, environment and genes always interact to produce the final product – the phenotype. What the behaviour geneticist wants to know is the relative contribution of each, the evolutionary history of the behavioural trait, and the underlying molecular, biochemical, and physiological mechanisms that mediate the expression of the behaviour.

QUANTITATIVE GENETICS

There are a number of basic methods used by behavioural geneticists which range from the simple to the almost intractable. Mendel's law of segregation illustrates how any character (or phenotype) that is determined by a single locus (a position on a chromosome at which a gene is situated) will segregate in a $3:1$ ratio in the F_2 (second filial) generation, assuming complete dominance of one of the alleles (an allele is simply one form of a gene). Mendel worked out his law of segregation using pea plant characteristics. Some behavioural characters show similar patterns of inheritance, for example the *waltzer* mutant mice which are neurologically abnormal, and behaviourally uncoordinated, and thus appear to "waltz". However, most naturally occurring behavioural differences that are observed between different people or different animals will not be due to single genetic differences, and the study of these behavioural characters requires the discipline of quantitative genetics.

One way of determining the approximate number of genes that might be determining a difference in a behavioural phenotype is to use a selection experiment. Starting from a genetically variable strain which is heterozygous at many loci, the organisms under study (usually flies, mice, or rats) are selected simultaneously for both high and low levels of a particular trait (aggression, sex drive, intelligence), and then bred together for several or many generations, selecting at each cycle. Imagine that after a few generations a peak and a depth of performance is reached in the two bidirectionally selected lines and no amount of subsequent selection can elevate or reduce the performance. This would argue that perhaps only one or two genes were segregating in the founder populations, and that they very soon became homozygous during the selection procedure. If the response to selection is slow, and small improvements and decrements are continually being made at every generation of selection, then it is clear that many genes are involved in the behavioural character under study. These genes will be continually "reshuffled" with the meiotic recombination that occurs during sexual reproduction and realigned within the "high" and "low" strains.

Imagine two highly inbred strains of animals, say mice. They have been maintained by brother–sister mating for many years and so each can be considered to be homozygous at every gene locus. The two lines show differences in the level of a particular behaviour, let us say aggression. By measuring the behavioural scores of progeny of the F_1, F_2, and the two back-crosses (where the F_1 is crossed back to each parent), it is possible by using simple mathematics to extract some very useful information about what is called the "genetic architecture" of a behavioural trait. This information includes the additive genetic component, A, the dominance component D, and the environmental component, E. To illustrate what "additive" and "dominance" mean, imagine two strains of mice; one has an aggression score of 10 arbitrary units and the other of zero. If the F_1 hybrid between the two strains had a mean score of 5 units then there is complete additivity. If the hybrids produce a score of 6 units then the deviation from the mean value is $6 - 5 = 1$ giving a dominance value of $+1$ unit. If we examine the phenotypic variances from the different crosses, we can obtain a measure of the genetic component of variation V_G (which is the additive genetic component V_A plus the dominance component V_D) and of the environmental variation V_E. Thus, the phenotypic variation that we see in a trait, V_P, equals

$$V_P = V_A + V_D + V_E$$

and the heritability (h^2) of a character is the ratio of the genetic variation to the total phenotypic variation:

$$h^2 = V_G / V_P.$$

This is sometimes called the broad heritability (h_B^2). The narrow heritability (h_N^2) is the ratio of the additive genetic variation divided by the total phenotypic variation:

$$h_N^2 = V_A / V_P.$$

h_N^2 is an important statistic for animal and plant breeders, because if a character has a high narrow heritability there are presumably lots of genes available that produce predictable additive effects. Thus two large animals should produce large progeny of intermediate size between them. The dominance component V_D is an irritant to the breeder, because it is pushing scores towards one or other parent unpredictably, because of segregation. Thus for selection experiments to work, a reasonable amount of predictable additive genetic variation must be present.

There are more sophisticated crossing schemes available for obtaining measures of V_A, V_D, V_E, such as the diallel cross and the triple test cross. The triple test cross, for example, can estimate the epistatic genetic component, which is the non-additive interaction of alleles at more than one locus. Let us take locus A' which can have allele A or a and locus B' which can have allele B or b. If certain combinations of these alleles produce completely unpredictable phenotypic scores, then epistatis or gene interactions are occurring.

The quantitative methods are an art in themselves and have reached high levels of complexity. The one thing that should always be borne in mind, however, from the simplest F_1, F_2 and back-cross method to the most esoteric multivariate path technique, is that all these analyses have implicit assumptions that are often unrealistic.

METHODOLOGY FOR HUMANS

Allied to these quantitative models are the three major methods used for human behavioural genetic analyses, which are twin, family, and adoption studies. As an example let us take the intelligence quotient, IQ. If you measured the IQ of pairs of monozygotic (MZ) twins and compared them with pairs of fraternal or dizygotic (DZ) twins, then if IQ has a heritable component, the MZ correlation should be greater than the DZ correlation. This is because MZ twins share all their genes, whereas DZ twins share on average only half their genetic endowment. However, it must be remembered that MZ twins have a more uniform uterine environment than DZ twins, and may also be treated more similarly than DZ twins within their family, because they look more similar and because they are always of the same sex. Thus it is conceivable that the more similar environment enjoyed by MZ twins from conception onwards may be the cause of more similar phenotypic scores in MZ compared to DZ twins. However, such evidence as exists concerning the possibility of more equal postnatal environments for MZ over DZ twins is equivocal (reviewed in Plomin et al., 1990).

Related to the twin method is the family study, where the similarities in the behavioural phenotype between two individuals of known genetic relatedness are compared. The parent/offspring correlation in IQ or any other character is underscored by a coefficient of genetic relatedness of .50 which reflects the number of genes shared by father or mother and each child. Siblings also share an average of half their genomes whereas grandparents with grandchildren have a coefficient of relatedness of .25. Half siblings, who share one parent only, like the grandparent/grandchild case, enjoy a coefficient of .25. Thus if we correlate IQ scores between fathers and sons, for example, and there is a strong heritable component to IQ, then the correlation should be higher than that between first cousins, who share .125 of their genomes. The first step in trying to assess whether genetic differences give phenotypic differences in human behaviour is to examine family relationships. If the correlation does not improve with the increasing degree of relatedness, then it is unlikely that the genetic component is significant.

The third method in human behaviour genetics is the adoption method. Here we are interested in unrelated individuals who live together, usually an adopted child and its non-biological parents. Any phenotypic correlation will be due to their shared home environment. A second relevant group is represented by genetically related individuals who for one reason or another are separated early in life and are raised in different families. However, in both these cases there are some complications. Perhaps an adoption agency selectively places a child into a "suitable" family, or perhaps identical twins are raised apart, but in two related families, for example one twin in an aunt's home and the other in the mother's. Perhaps such shared familial situations tend to make these twins more similar than they might otherwise have been.

Let us now turn to some of the important behavioural phenotypes that have been analysed in humans. What we would like to do eventually is to isolate the genes for high IQ, for example, or for extraversion and introversion as another example, and find out what types of proteins these genes encode. Regrettably this is not possible at present with humans.

HUMAN BEHAVIOUR GENETICS

The behavioural phenotypes that are commonly studied are cognitive abilities such as IQ, and the psychopathologies such as schizophrenia and unipolar and bipolar depression. However, a range of other personality variables have also been studied, together with such talents as musical ability, creativity, and so on.

Intelligence IQ

A large number of twin studies have been performed, including the famous (or infamous) studies of Cyril Burt. Burt's results have been challenged and are generally believed to be fraudulent. I refer any interested reader to a critical review of the whole affair by Joynson (1989). However, the fact that one of a large number of twin studies may not be reliable does not weaken the conclusions that are obtained from examining the results of all the other twin studies. Clearly IQ variation has a considerable genetic component. Figure 1 summarizes the IQ correlations taken from studies of various family relationships and reviewed by Bouchard and McGue (1981). MZ twins have a correlation in IQ that clusters around .85 whereas DZ twins have correlations ranging from .50 to .70, which is slightly higher than that for full siblings. The difference between the correlation for DZ twins (.60) and siblings (.47) suggest that DZ twins, because of their age similarity, have a more similar environment than ordinary siblings. (In Figure 1 "midparent IQ" is the average of the parents' IQ; "midoffspring IQ" is the average of the off-spring's IQ.) From Figure 1 we can see that one or two of the correlations are not quite what would be predicted based on a simple additive genetic model with no environmental influence. Siblings reared apart should have a higher correlation in IQ than .24, perhaps as high as .50. Although only two of these studies are reported, the apparent significant environmental contribution implied is amply supported by the last four sets of correlations in Figure 1, which are taken from adoption studies. Significant correlations between .19 and .29 again reflect the environmental contribution to IQ scores.

The difference between MZ and DZ correlations is about .26 (.86 − .60) and reflects half the genetic variation in IQ (because DZ twins share half their genes whereas MZ twins share all their genes). By doubling this figure we obtain an approximate broad heritability of .52. Thus the conclusion from all these studies is that about half the phenotypic variation in IQ is due to genetic differences, and half to environment. Can we isolate or even count the number of genes involved? Not directly. However, in a mammal about 70 per cent of all genes are expressed in the nervous system (John & Miklos, 1988). This tells us that natural selection invests a huge amount in brains. We might consider that the most conservative estimate of the number of human

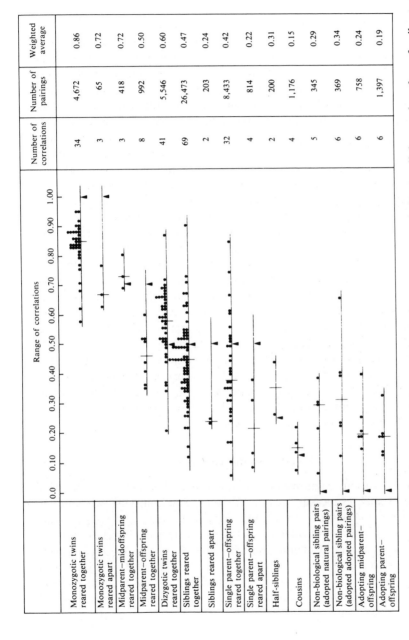

	Number of correlations	Number of pairings	Weighted average
Monozygotic twins reared together	34	4,672	0.86
Monozygotic twins reared apart	3	65	0.72
Midparent–midoffspring reared together	3	418	0.72
Midparent–offspring reared together	8	992	0.50
Dizygotic twins reared together	41	5,546	0.60
Siblings reared together	69	26,473	0.47
Siblings reared apart	2	203	0.24
Single parent–offspring reared together	32	8,433	0.42
Single parent–offspring reared apart	4	814	0.22
Half-siblings	2	200	0.31
Cousins	4	1,176	0.15
Non-biological sibling pairs (adopted natural pairings)	5	345	0.29
Non-biological sibling pairs (adopted adopted pairings)	6	369	0.34
Adopting midparent–offspring	6	758	0.24
Adopting parent–offspring	6	1,397	0.19

Figure 1 Synopsis of Bouchard and McGue's (1981) presentation of the IQ correlation coefficients taken from family, twin, and adoption studies up to 1980. Vertical lines show the median correlation coefficient and the arrows give the correlation expected if IQ variation were completely due to additive genetic variation with no environmental component.

Source: Reproduced from Plomin, Defries, and McClearn, 1990, and based on Bouchard and McGue, 1981. Reproduced with permission from both sources

7

genes is 100,000. Consequently up to 70,000 of these genes might be expressed in the nervous system, and we could imagine that many of these genes have a function. Furthermore, we know from molecular population genetic analysis that all of these genes would be represented by more than one allele at the DNA level. Some of this variation in DNA sequence will be "silent" and not produce any amino acid changes in brain cell proteins. Some of these DNA variants will be neutral and change the amino acid sequence but with no effect on the proteins being produced. However, some variants will alter the amino acid sequence and perhaps also alter the activity of the nerve cell proteins. Therefore if 10 per cent of these genes have different alleles segregating in the population and 10 per cent of these alleles in turn give changes in the nervous system, then perhaps 700 genes will be potentially contributing to differences in neural performance and inevitably to IQ. Not all of these hypothetical 700 genes will be segregating within the native British or American population, but by even these conservative estimates it is obvious that many genes will be contributing to the variation we see in IQ: some of these genes will push IQ scores up and some will push them down.

While at present we cannot hope to identify or isolate IQ genes that are segregating in normal populations, can we nevertheless understand how the environment which determines fully half of IQ variation acts on the phenotype? A clue comes from Figure 1 where unrelated children raised together produce an overall correlation of .32. This does suggest that about one-third of the total IQ variation is due to the shared family environment. Several reports suggest that the influence of the shared environment drops sharply between the teenage and early adult years (Plomin, 1988). This implies that shared home environment is a significant influence on the heritability of IQ early in life, but recedes as children grow up and move to different environments. It is comforting therefore that these correlations reflect such intuitively "sensible" features in the development of young adults.

Developmental studies

In some investigations cognitive ability has been studied longitudinally with the children's abilities measured as they mature. The Louisville twin study is probably the best known (Wilson, 1983). For twenty years, 500 pairs of twins were tested at three-month intervals between the ages of 3 and 24 months using the Bayley Scales of mental and motor development. Various IQ tests were given at roughly one-year intervals from the ages of 3 to 9 years and then again at 15 years. Until the age of 6 months, the MZ twin correlation does not exceed that of DZ twins. By 3 years of age the difference is still small, .77 for MZ twins, .67 for DZ twins. The heritability of IQ increases until about the age of 6 years and then declines (Wilson, 1983; see also Figure 2). As genes are not transcribed constantly, but are switched on and off at different stages of development this may reflect an underlying temporal

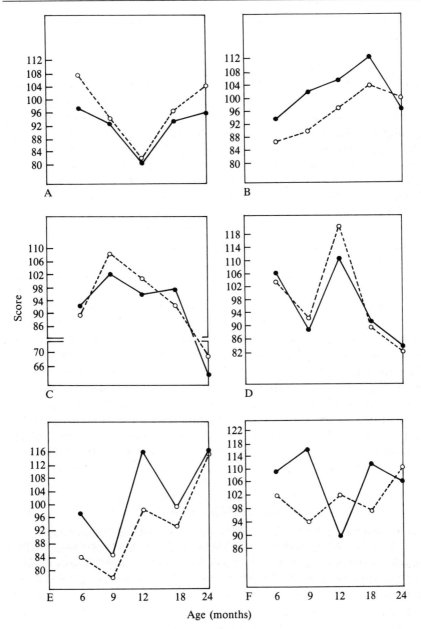

Figure 2 The mental development profiles for MZ twins between the ages of 6 and 24 months from the Louisville twin study (Wilson, 1983). The pairs A to E show high similarity whereas pair F does not

Source: Reproduced from Plomin et al., 1990, and based on Wilson, 1983. Reproduced with permission from both sources

regulation of neurally acting genes. Another well-known longitudinal study, the Colorado adoption project, was set up in 1975 (Plomin & Defries, 1985). The children are tested at yearly intervals with a battery of cognitive and physical tests, making this the most complete adoption project so far undertaken. Plomin, Defries and Fulker (1988) were able to confirm with their adoptees Wilson's (1983) twin study findings on the increase in heritability of IQ until middle childhood. A large number of multivariate analyses have been applied to this and other longitudinal projects. One can barely pick up an issue of the journal *Behavior Genetics* without finding yet another complex analytical technique being used. It is not appropriate to address these statistical models in this review, especially as I am not competent to make judgements on them. However, some of the basic features of these models and their results are described in Plomin et al.'s (1990) text.

Race and IQ

One cannot leave the subject of the genetic basis of IQ without some reference to the racial question, raised most prominently by Jensen. The average IQ difference between blacks and whites in the United States is about one standard deviation (or 15 IQ points). If the variance in IQ is at least partly genetic, could the difference between the two populations be genetic? Jensen (1972) argued that blacks may be genetically inferior in IQ to whites, and so the various government educational programmes that were set up with the intention of boosting scholastic achievement in disadvantaged children were doomed to failure. Jensen argued that because the heritability of IQ is high, there was little room left for the environment to improve performance. However, one could just as easily argue that short-sightedness is highly heritable, but can be corrected by using the appropriate environmental intervention, that is, by wearing glasses. Thus a highly heritable character need not be immune from improvement by the environment. The evidence presented for and against a predominantly genetic explanation of the racial differences in IQ is evenly balanced (see Loehlin, Lindzey, & Spuhler, 1975).

Behavioural genetic analyses have also been performed on more specific mental performance measures including verbal comprehension, fluency, reasoning, spatial abilities, school achievement, and reading (see Nichols, 1978). Generally the heritabilities for such behavioural indices are rather smaller than those for IQ.

Psychopathology

Schizophrenia

The second major behaviour genetic adventure with human subjects concerns the work with schizophrenia. Instead of correlating the scores of two relatives as one does for IQ, the investigator looks for concordances between relatives. If one twin has the disease, does the other? However, there are some intrinsic problems with the study of all psychopathologies. First, the diagnosis of schizophrenia can vary from country to country (Gottesman & Shields, 1982). Second, a subject may not have schizophrenia when tested, but might develop it later in life. Quantitative analysis is also difficult because one is not dealing with an absolute score as in IQ. Thus measures of heritability of schizophrenia are very approximate.

Gottesman and Shields (1982) reviewed the various family, twin, and adoption studies up to that period. While schizophrenia in the general population affects 1 per cent of people, the children of schizophrenics have a 10 per cent liability for the disease. From a variety of twin studies (Gottesman & Shields, 1982; Kendler & Robinette, 1983) the concordance rates for MZ twins varied from 31 to 58 per cent and from 6.5 to 27 per cent for DZ twins. Taking the lower figure of 31 per cent for MZ twins, this suggests a strong environmental component, as identical genotypes are, more often than not, discordant for schizophrenia. Doubling the difference between the MZ and DZ concordances gives a rough estimate of heritability which, depending on which studies you take, can approach .50.

Adoption studies

Heston (1966) examined the adopted-away children of 47 severely affected women. The children were raised in families free of any obvious psychopathology, but of the 47, 5 were clearly schizophrenic and another 4 showed schizophrenic symptoms. Thus 9 out of 47 of the children of the affected mothers could be considered to show some form of the disease. The control group of 50 adoptees of normal mothers gave no incidence of schizophrenic symptoms. These results, which confirm the genetic hypothesis, have been reproduced in a number of other studies.

Wender, Rosenthal, Kety, Schulsinger, and Welner (1974) reported a study in Denmark where adoptees whose biological parents were not schizophrenic were fostered in homes in which at least one of the parents was schizophrenic. The results showed that the schizophrenic environment itself was not enough to increase the prevalence of schizophrenia in the children. Wender, Rosenthal, and Kety (1968) compared three groups: biological parents raising their own schizophrenic children; adoptive parents rearing their schizophrenic adoptees; and adoptive parents rearing unaffected adoptees.

11

Higher frequencies of schizophrenia were found in the biological parents of schizophrenics compared to the adoptive parents of schizophrenics. However, these adoptive parents of schizophrenic children were given higher schizophrenia ratings than adoptive parents with unaffected children, suggesting that raising a schizophrenic child can produce schizophrenic symptoms in otherwise healthy parents.

Molecular genetics of psychopathologies

Since the late 1980s, the power of molecular genetics has been brought to bear on schizophrenia. Sherrington et al. (1988) raised the possibility that a dominant gene on chromosome 5 appeared to be involved in the appearance of schizophrenia in a number of Icelandic and English families. However, a number of subsequent studies failed to confirm this linkage of a major gene for schizophrenia to chromosome 5 (reviewed in Byerley, 1989). However, schizophrenia may show genetic heterogeneity in that several different major loci can mutate and each mutation can by itself produce schizophrenia. If different genes have been mutated in different families, the end point in all the families is similar, that is, a high incidence of schizophrenia. Pedigree analysis of different families would then produce exactly the type of apparently contradictory findings mentioned above.

Similar inconsistencies appear in the molecular genetic literature for manic depression. Egeland et al. (1987) reported that within the reproductively isolated Amish community of Pennsylvania, a gene linked to the tip of the short arm of chromosome 11 appeared to be implicated in the high incidence of bipolar depression. However, further analysis of these data failed to confirm the linkage to chromosome 11 and studies of other pedigrees also excluded chromosome 11. Still further investigations have suggested that manic depression may be linked to the X chromosome (reviewed by Robertson, 1989; Gershon, Martineo, Goldin, & Gejman, 1990; Hodgkinson, Mullan, & Gurling 1990). The conclusion forced upon us is that manic depression represents a genetically heterogeneous set of syndromes with a similar phenotypic end-point. However, what is beyond doubt is that manic depressive psychosis has a strong genetic component as demonstrated from the results of twin, family, and adoption studies (see Plomin et al., 1990, for a review).

Family, twin, and adoption studies have also been applied to alcoholism, delinquency, and various forms of antisocial behaviour. In these psychopathologies, as in childhood hyperactivity, extraversion and neuroticism, musical ability, and sexual orientation, significant genetic components are implicated. In fact it is difficult to escape the conclusion that genetic variation plays a very important role in just about every form of behaviour that has been studied.

ANIMAL BEHAVIOUR GENETICS

Historically, there have been two major schools of thought in animal behaviour genetics. One school is interested in the genetic analysis of behaviour and its evolutionary implications. The other approach has sought to use genetic analysis to study the neural mechanisms that underlie behaviour. Thus the evolutionary school tends to concentrate on polygenic characters, while the neurobiological school focuses more on single genes. It has become quite clear over the years that single genes have quite a lot to offer in the understanding of behaviour from an evolutionary perspective.

Interspecific studies

One way of analysing behaviour that may have a genetic basis is to examine fixed-action patterns, instinctive behavioural elements which may be relatively unmodified by experience and therefore easy to study genetically. If two species show a difference in behaviour, and can be crossed together to obtain F_1 and F_2 and back-cross progeny, then simple Mendelian ratios will reflect the existence of a single gene difference in behaviour. Examples of this are few and far between. Interspecific genetics is difficult precisely because of the reproductive barriers that have evolved to keep the species' gene pools apart. However, molecular techniques now allow us to move a gene from species A to species B and observe the consequences. I shall discuss below the potential of this exciting new methodology for analysing species-specific behaviour.

Intra-species comparisons

A more fruitful approach is to examine different inbred strains within a species. The genetic architecture (as discussed above) has been obtained for many different behavioural characteristics in many different organisms, for example aggression, locomotor activity, emotional behaviour, sexual behaviour, learning ability, and so on – the list is almost endless. Rarely is it that a single gene determines the difference in behaviour between two strains of mice, for example, and quantitative methods can be used to examine the contributions of the additive genetic component A, the dominance component D, etc. I mentioned earlier that if there is plenty of additive genetic variation then it is easy to select for high or low levels of a character. Imagine now that natural selection has done the job for us on a characteristic, such as rapid learning ability in flies, so that smart flies are "fitter" and selected over dumb ones. What shall we see in the genetic architecture for learning in these flies? We should see an absence of additive genetic variation as natural selection has "used up" the variation in the additively acting "smart" genes.

I shall give one classic example of this approach. Fulker (1966) studied the mating propensity of male fruit flies from several inbred lines which differed in the average number of females mated per unit time. Male mating behaviour is a major fitness character and would be expected to be under strong selection for high levels of sexual performance. Using the diallel cross method, Fulker indeed showed that the additive component was low compared to the dominance component. This is one of the first applications of the diallel cross to behaviour, and fortunately it came up with a reasonable answer, thereby verifying the method. Many different types of similar experiments have been performed and space does not permit a detailed discussion of these experiments. Instead I refer the interested reader to the relevant sections of Hay's (1985) text.

Artificial selection studies can also produce estimates of heritability. Most behaviours respond to selection, and again, large numbers of studies have been reported, especially on invertebrates because the generation time is so much faster than mammals. A character that shows a rapid response to selection in both the high and low direction, as in Tryon's (1940) experiment, suggests that the character is probably determined by one or a few segregating genes. A more measured response, such as that obtained by Manning (1961) in his selection study for fast and slow fruit fly mating, implies that many genes are contributing to the phenotype. An asymmetric response to selection, as also obtained by Manning, where he obtained a response for slow mating but not for fast mating, is also informative. It suggests that natural selection has already selected the additively acting genes that determine fast mating, and it is therefore difficult to improve on this "ceiling" with further selection.

Selection experiments together with inter-strain analyses produce a useful picture of genetic architecture and invoke the past evolutionary history of a behavioural trait. Identifying specific genes in a polygenic system is difficult and has usually been limited to calculating the contributions to the phenotypic variation of the different chromosomes. This can be performed quite readily in the fruit fly where it is possible to track intact chromosomes through several generations without having the inconvenience of recombination. For example, a fly's third chromosome from strain B can be placed into a background where chromosomes 1, 2 and 4 are from strain A and the hybrid fly can be examined to see whether the B chromosome produces B-like behaviour. This has been used in many studies and is the first step in identifying specific genes within a polygenic system. To identify and map polygenes that determine behavioural differences between strains requires many markers on each chromosome to which linkage of the behavioural genes can be assigned. Polymorphic molecular markers have been developed, which are pieces of DNA that differ between strain A and B, and linkage of the behavioural phenotype to the markers can be performed using standard segregation analysis.

14

Single genes and behaviour

A simpler way forward is to analyse behaviour by using single gene mutations. For example, the *ebony* gene in *Drosophila melanogaster* affects body colour, visual behaviour, sexual behaviour, and locomotor activity (Kyriacou, Burnet, & Connolly 1978; Kyriacou, 1985). The biochemical lesion induced in *ebony* mutants obviously affects the pathway that is recruited in the normal expression of all these different phenotypes. Thus *ebony* is a pleiotropic gene. Molecular analysis of the *ebony* gene reveals that it encodes an enzyme required both for the normal tanning of the cuticle (hence the dark body colour in the mutant), and also in nervous tissue (hence the behavioural defects). Furthermore, *ebony* is of interest to evolutionary biologists because *ebony* mutants are found in nature even though the mutants themselves mate poorly given their visual defect (males cannot follow the female during the courtship display). Yet heterozygous *ebony* males are at a significant mating advantage to both the wild-type and *ebony* mutants, and therefore the *ebony* gene continues to segregate in natural and artificial laboratory populations (Kyriacou, 1985). This hybrid vigour in the sexual behaviour of the heterozygotes maintains the *ebony* polymorphism (Kyriacou, 1985), and has evolutionary implications as it maintains genetic variation at the *ebony* locus. Examples of morphological mutations like *ebony*, which are of relevance to psychologists and evolutionary biologists, are rather rare.

Single gene mutations in mice include about 300 that affect neurological functioning, for example *waltzer*, *twirler*, *reeler*, etc. These mice were highly prized in Victorian times for their bizarre behaviours, and the mutants have given some insights into cerebellar, inner ear, and neural crest development. However, the interest in these "behavioural" genes is at present developmental rather than psychological (Hay, 1985).

A breakthrough in single gene research came when Seymour Benzer (1973) advocated the use of mutagenesis and mass screening techniques in order to induce new mutations in the behavioural systems of choice. *Drosophila* was ideally suited to such a venture and Benzer, using ingenious devices and amusing names for his new mutants, induced neurological mutants (*ether-a-go-go*, *drop dead*), sexual behaviour mutations (*coitus interruptus*), flight and visual mutants, etc. He also extended a technique called "fate-mapping" to locate the primary anatomical site of action of a mutant gene. After the first generation of mutations had been produced, some of Benzer's students began to study complex behavioural phenotypes, such as learning, biological rhythmicity, and courtship behaviour.

Learning

The demonstration that flies could be classically conditioned en masse to

15

associate electric shock with odour laid the foundation for the subsequent isolation of mutant flies which learned poorly or failed to learn at all (Quinn & Greenspan, 1984). Several such mutants, *dunce* (*dnc*), *rutabaga* (*rut*), *amnesiac* (*amn*), *turnip* (*tur*), etc., also showed defects in other tests that were designed to measure aspects of learning mediated by different sensory modalities (see Kyriacou & Hall, 1993, for review). This suggested that the mutations were acting centrally within the nervous system because more than one sensory modality was affected. Biochemical and molecular characterization of *dnc* and *rut* (see Davis & Dauwalder, 1991) revealed that these genes encoded enzymes from the cyclic adenose monophosphate (cAMP) second messenger signalling system. This is particularly interesting as the cAMP pathway appears to be implicated in the cellular mechanisms that underlie learning in the mollusc *Aplysia*, much studied by Kandel and his colleagues. The *dnc* gene appears to be expressed particularly prominently in the region of the fly brain known as the mushroom bodies (Davis & Dauwalder, 1991). Surgical lesion of these regions in higher insects such as the hymenoptera leads to memory defects (Erber, Masuhr, & Menzel, 1980).

In addition, the number of mushroom body fibres rises in the first week of the adult fly's life (see Balling, Technau, & Heisenberg, 1987). Flies raised in a sensory deprived environment show reduction in the number of these fibres compared to flies raised in an enriched environment. However, *dnc* and *rut* mutants do not show this experience-dependent increase in fibre number when raised in enriched and deprived environments. Consequently, these learning mutants have helped to identify the biochemical cellular, and anatomical substrates of learning, and have been shown to be involved in the critical periods when sensory experiences can mould the fly's brain. Flies are evidently not born knowing all they need to know.

Biological rhythms

In 1971 Konopka and Benzer induced three mutations that altered the periodicity of the fly's circadian clock. The three mutations shortened, lengthened, or obliterated the fly's 24-hour rhythmic behaviour as measured by pupal to adult eclosion and locomotor activity cycles (Konopka & Benzer, 1971; see also Figure 3). All three mutations mapped to the same spot on the X chromosome, in other words, they were all alleles of a single locus which was called the *period* (*per*) gene. Thus the *per^s* variant has a short 19-hour cycle, *per^{L1}* mutant has a long 29-hour rhythm, and the *per^{01}* fly is arrhythmic (see Figure 3). The three mutations also disrupt a one-minute (ultradian) cycle found in the male's courtship song: *per^s* males have a short 40-second cycle, *per^{L1}* males have a long 80-second cycle and *per^{01}* males are arrhythmic (Kyriacou & Hall, 1993). Finally the *per* mutants also affect the fly's 10-day egg-to-adult developmental cycle in a predictable manner with *per^s* mutants developing faster than the wild-type and *per^{L1}* mutants

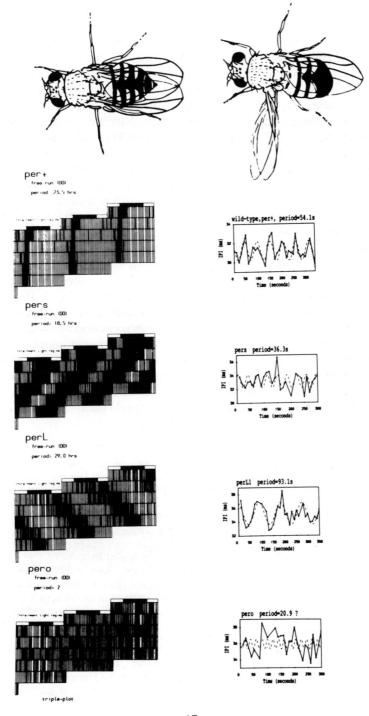

developing more slowly, while per^{01} mutants give a somewhat erratic profile (Kyriacou & Hall, 1993). Thus the *per* gene appears to control biological timing in a rather general way. The *per* gene was cloned and sequenced (see Kyriacou & Hall, 1993, for review) and encodes a 1,200-amino-acid protein of unknown function. It has some similarities to two other proteins that are believed to act as transcription factors. Transcription factors are proteins that act to switch on or off other genes. The *per* messenger RNA (mRNA) cycles in abundance with a circadian period, as does the *per* protein (mRNA is the molecule that enables protein to be synthesized from a gene). There is good evidence that the *per* protein feeds back on itself and negatively regulates its own mRNA transcription. Consequently the current model of *per's* action is as follows. As the *per* protein is made it reaches a critical concentration, and then blocks more of its own mRNA transcription. As the mRNA is blocked, so less protein is translated, giving the mRNA and protein cycles that are observed. Imagine now that *per* encodes a transcription factor which turns on or off all the other downstream genes required to get the animal behaving rhythmically. As the *per* protein waxes and wanes, batteries of these genes will be turned on or off in unison, giving circadian cycling of many different behaviours. The per^s protein achieves its critical concentration 5 hours earlier than the wild-type *per* protein because it may be more stable, and the per^{L1} protein 5 hours later than the normal protein because it may be less stable. In per^{01} mutants the *per* protein is truncated to 450 amino acids and therefore must have very low activity.

The *per* gene is expressed in many organs of the fly and in fact many of these structures have been shown in the past to have circadian cycles in their physiology (see Hall & Kyriacou, 1990). The *per* gene is expressed in the

---

Figure 3 The phenotypic effects of the *per* mutants in *Drosophila melanogaster*. The locomotor activity profile (actogram) is given on the left and the song cycle on the right. The activity data are triple plotted with day 1 on the top row, days 1 and 2 on the next row, days 1, 2, and 3 on the next, with days 2, 3, and 4, then 3, 4, and 5, then 4, 5, and 6, etc. on the subsequent rows. Each vertical line represents the amount of activity in a 30-minute time bin. The darker the shade the more intense the activity. The flies were allowed to "free-run" in constant darkness after first being maintained in a 12-hour light, 12-hour dark environmental light cycle. The times of lights on and off before the free-run are represented by the horizontal black and white lines above the actogram. Note how the wild-type (per^+) fly becomes active at about the same time each day, whereas the per^s mutant begins activity at approximately 5 hours earlier each day, and the per^{L1} mutant about 5 hours later. The per^{01} mutant is arrhythmic (insomniac!). To the right are presented the song rhythms of the males carrying the different *per* alleles. The males wing vibration produces pulses (see also legend to Figure 4) with an interpulse interval (IPI) which oscillates with a *period* of approximately 55 seconds in per^+, 36 seconds in per^s, 93 seconds in per^{L1}, and a weak non-significant 21-second cycle is obtained in per^{01}. The plots represent the mean IPIs for each 10 seconds of time for about 5 minutes of courtship

brain and visual system of the fly, and certain cells called "lateral" neurons appear to be particularly important in mediating circadian locomotor activity. Thus the marriage of behaviour and molecular biology has, in this case, produced a real insight into the cellular mechanisms that are involved in determining one of life's ubiquitous features.

Sexual behaviour

The courtship song cycle of male fruit flies (Figure 3) is also affected by the *per* mutations mentioned above (Kyriacou & Hall, 1989). The song cycle is functionally important and a 60-second cycle appears to enhance the *D. melanogaster*'s female's receptivity, while a 35-second cycle will enhance a *D. simulans* female's receptivity to *D. simulans* males (Kyriacou & Hall, 1986). Males from *D. simulans* (which is a closely related sympatric species to *D. melanogaster*) sing with a 35-second cycle. Thus the song cycle may act as part of a species recognition mechanism with the different species of *Drosophila* females preferring the song cycles of their conspecific males. Interspecific crosses reveal that the species difference in song cycles between *D. melanogaster* and *D. simulans* (60 seconds versus 35 seconds) map to the *X* chromosome. This suggests that perhaps it is the sex-linked (*X* chromosome) *per* gene, that may differ in the two species and be causing the behavioural difference between them. This was confirmed by taking the cloned *D. simulans per* gene and transforming it into a *D. melanogaster per^{01}* arrhythmic mutant (Wheeler et al., 1991). Not only were locomotor activity cycles restored in the transgenic *per^{01} D. melanogaster* fly, but also the song cycle produced by the transgenic males revealed the 40-second *D. simulans* rhythm. Thus the species-specific behaviour of one species (*D. simulans*) was transferred to another (*D. melanogaster*) by shunting one gene between the two species. This remarkable result shows that an apparently complex species-specific sexual behaviour, which may by its nature be implicated in speciation, can be determined by a single gene. A song cycle is superimposed upon the basic structure of the courtship song. Males vibrate their wings and produce a series of pulses with interpulse intervals (IPI) that are on average 30–40 ms (milliseconds) in *D. melanogaster* and 40–60 ms in *D. simulans* (Kyriacou & Hall, 1986; see also Figure 4). These IPI lengths cycle with the *per* determined period in the two species. However, two mutations also affect the characteristics of the song structure itself. The *cacophony* (*cac*) and *dissonance* (*diss*) mutations, both which are sex-linked (Kulkarni & Hall, 1987; Kulkarni, Steinlauf, & Hall, 1988) lead to abnormal pulses being produced (Figure 4). The *cac* pulses are polycyclic and have a large amplitude, while *diss* pulses may be monocyclic at the beginning of a song burst but degenerate, becoming polycyclic towards the end, often with an increasing amplitude (see Figure 4). The *cac* and *diss* mutations map to two independent loci, both of which have other mutant alleles that affect vision. Thus *cac* is

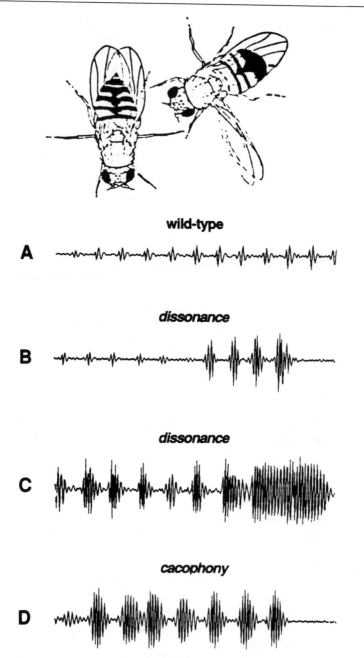

Figure 4 The song pulses of wild-type, *dissonance* (diss) and *cacophony* (cac) mutant males
Source: Reproduced from Kyriacou, 1990, and based on Kulkarni et al., 1988. Reproduced with permission from both sources

a mutant allele of a gene called *L(1)L13* which has another mutant allele called *night-blind-A (nbA)* (Kulkarni & Hall, 1987). The *diss* mutation is a mutant allele of the *no-on-transient A (nonA)* locus, but *nonA* mutants have defective vision but normal songs (Rendahl, Jones, Kulkarni, Bagully, & Hall, 1992), whereas the *diss* mutant does have a visual defect (Kulkarni & Hall, 1987). The *diss* mutation is now formally designated as *nonA*^{diss} to show that it is a mutant allele of the *nonA* locus. The *nonA* gene has been cloned and sequenced (Jones & Rubin, 1990) and it appears to encode a protein that may be able to bind to RNA. Such proteins can play a regulatory role and often show rapid evolution between species (Kyriacou, 1992). However, this does not give us any biochemical insight into the possible nature of the *diss* protein. It is remarkable, however, that two different song mutants, *cac* and *diss*, are both alleles of visual loci, demonstrating a neurogenetic connection between the visual and song mechanisms during development.

Drosophila, for many, is the organism of choice because its genetics and molecular biology is well developed compared to the mouse, for example, and its behaviour is complex enough to interest a psychologist and a zoologist. The nematode worm *Caenorhabdytis elegans* also has a lot to offer the neurogeneticist in that its molecular biology and genetics are as well understood as that of the fly. The nematode's behaviour, however, is much simpler than *Drosophila* but for studying the development of the nervous system the nematode is in a league of its own (Way, 1990). This is because the development of each of the worm's neurons has been documented in detail. Behaviour such as touch reception has been analysed using mutations; more recently rhythmic behaviour has also come under scrutiny. Perhaps by the turn of the millennium someone will be able to teach the nematodes to learn, opening up the neuromolecular dissection of learning in a very simple nervous system.

Aplysia egg-laying behaviour

The molecular analysis of the egg-laying behaviour of *Aplysia* has provided some major insights into the control of complex behaviours. Egg laying is a highly stereotyped behaviour pattern and is expressed sequentially (see Figure 5). The behaviour consists of a change in the locomotor activity and eating patterns of the snail and an increase in its heart and breathing rate. The oviduct extrudes a string of eggs which the mouth grasps, and with a series of side-to-side movements the egg string is pulled out by the mouth. Mucus is secreted on to the eggs, and with a final head movement the eggs are deposited on a solid substrate (see Figure 5). The complete sequence of this highly stereotyped behaviour pattern can be generated by injecting an extract, which is produced from two clusters of neurons positioned above the abdominal ganglion, the "bag" cells. The factor that produces this complex

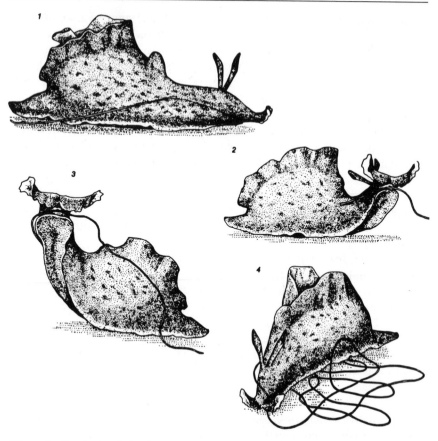

Figure 5 Egg-laying behaviour in *Aplysia*. The egg string is extruded by contractions of the oviduct (1), is placed in the mouth (2), and mucus is secreted on the string with side-to-side head movements, while the string is being drawn out (3). The egg string is finally deposited on a substrate (4)

Source: From "How Genes Control an Innate Behaviour" Richard Scheller and Richard Axel. Copyright © March 1984 by Scientific American, Inc. All rights reserved.

behavioural repertoire is a 36-amino-acid peptide called egg-laying hormone (ELH). Scheller and Axel (1984) were able to clone the gene for ELH (see Figure 6). When they examined the DNA sequence they found that it potentially encoded several different peptides, one of which was ELH, but also three others α, β, and acidic peptides. In fact the gene, once translated into the precursor polypeptide, could potentially release ten or eleven different peptides. Scheller realized that if different patterns of peptides could be released from this precursor protein, then a huge combination of different behaviours could be switched on in the snail. Imagine that each of the peptides can alter the firing patterns of the different neurons important for the expression of the egg-laying-behaviour repertoire. The potential for a

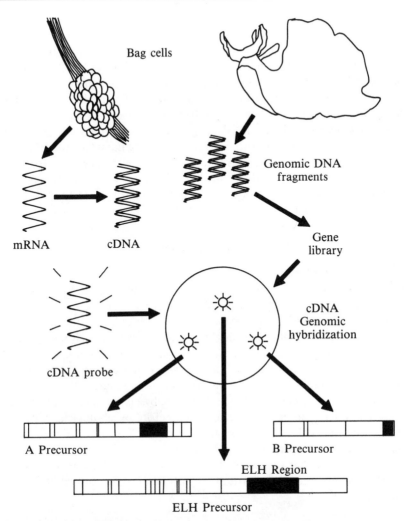

§QFigure 6 Isolation of the *Aplysia ELH* gene family. The bag cells produce messenger RNA (mRNA) which is used to make the complementary double-stranded DNA (cDNA). This cDNA molecule acts as a probe when labelled with a radioisotope. The genomic DNA from *Aplysia* is cut with restriction enzymes into small pieces and the fragments are recombined with a vector (a plasmid or virus) to form a gene library. The genomic DNA fragments can then be probed with the cDNA, which will hybridize to any complementary DNA and light it up. Three positives are obtained which encoded the *ELH*, A, and B precursor peptides (see text). The *ELH* peptide is represented in the *ELH* precursor as the darker shading. Similar regions are also present in the A and B precursors (see text)

Source: Reproduced with permission from Kyriacou, 1990

precursor protein to generate complex behaviour is enormous with over 1,000 combinations of different peptides possible. This work with *Aplysia* was the first application of molecular biology to complex behaviour. A strong evolutionary component is also present in this investigation, as Scheller and Axel (1984) originally found three similar genes, the *ELH* precursor gene, and the *A* and *B* precursor genes (see Figure 6). The *A* and *B* peptides were produced in the atrial gland and appeared to control the release of *ELH*. The fact that the gene sequences of the *ELH*, *A*, and *B* genes were similar, suggested that they evolved by a process of duplication of the original ancestral *ELH* gene. The *A* and *B* genes began to diverge from the *ELH* gene, and from each other, eventually taking on different, but related regulatory function. Other *Aplysia* species do not have *A* and *B* genes, suggesting that the *ELH* locus indeed represents the ancestral DNA.

CONCLUSIONS

Genetic analysis of behaviour can be performed at many different levels, from the evolutionary to the biochemical. With humans, the methods used are limited to making statements about whether a particular behavioural phenotype has a genetic component or not. With animals, the whole range of genetic, biochemical, physiological, and molecular techniques can be applied to answer penetrating questions about the evolution and the neural control of a behavioural pattern. In the twenty-first century it appears that molecular neurobiology will become the major life science. No one scientist can possibly be an expert in all the different subjects that are required for an integrated understanding of behaviour. Therefore psychologists, zoologists, biochemists, molecular biologists, and geneticists will have to begin to formulate ways of communicating with each other, free of the jargon peculiar to their own particular speciality. They have a lot to offer one another, and I hope that my modest contribution in these pages contributes to the dialogue.

FURTHER READING

Fuller, J. L., & Thompson, W. R. (1978). *Foundations of behavior genetics*. St Louis, MO: Mosby.

Greenspan, R. J. (Ed.) (1990). Genetics in the study of the nervous system. *Seminars in the Neuroscience, 12*(3), 143–241.

Hall, J. C. (1982). Genetics of the nervous system in *Drosophila. Quarterly Review of Biophysics, 15,* 223–479.

Plomin, R. (1990). The role of inheritance in behavior. *Science, 248,* 183–188.

Vogler, G. P. (Ed.) (1992). Human developmental behaviour genetics. *Behavior Genetics, 22*(2), 189–244.

REFERENCES

Balling, A., Technau, G. M., & Heisenberg, M. (1987). Are the structural changes in adult *Drosophila* mushroom bodies memory traces? Studies in biochemical learning mutants. *Journal of Neurogenetics, 4,* 64–73.

Benzer, S. (1973). Genetic dissection of behavior. *Scientific American, 229*(6), 24–37.

Bouchard, T. J. Jr, & McGue, M. (1981). Familial studies of intelligence: A review. *Science, 212,* 1055–1059.

Byerley, W. F. (1989). Genetic linkage revisited. *Nature, 340,* 340–341.

Davis, R. L., & Dauwalder, B. (1991). The *Drosophila dunce* locus: Learning and memory genes in the fly. *Trends in Genetics, 7,* 224–229.

Egeland, J. A., Gerhardt, D. S., Pauls, D. L., Sussex, J. N., Kidd, K. K., Allen, C. K., Hosteller, A. M., & Housman, D. E. (1987). Bipolar affective disorders linked to DNA markers on chromosome 11. *Nature, 325,* 783–787.

Erber, J., Masuhr, R., & Menzel, R. (1980). Localization of short-term memory in bee (*Apis mellifera*). *Physiological Entomology, 5,* 343–358.

Fulker, D. W. (1966). Mating speed in male *Drosphila melanogaster*: A psychogenetic analysis. *Science, 153,* 203–205.

Galton, F. (1869). *Hereditary genius: An inquiry into its laws and consequences.* London: Macmillan.

Gershon, E. S., Martineo, M., Goldin, L. R., & Gejman, P. V. (1990). Genetic mapping of common diseases. The challenges of manic-depressive illness and schizophrenia. *Trends in Genetics, 6,* 282–287.

Gottesman, I. I., & Shields, J. (1982). *Schizophrenia: The epigenetic puzzle.* Cambridge: Cambridge University Press.

Hall, J. C., & Kyriacou, C. P. (1990). Genetics of biological rhythms in *Drosophila*. *Advances in Insect Physiology, 22,* 221–298.

Hay, D. A. (1985). *Essentials of behaviour genetics.* Oxford: Basil Blackwell.

Heston, L. L. (1966). Psychiatric disorders in foster home reared children of schizophrenic mothers. *British Journal Psychiatry, 112,* 819–825.

Hodgkinson, S., Mullan, M. J., & Gurling, H. M. D. (1990). The role of genetic factors in the etiology of the affective disorders. *Behavior Genetics, 20,* 235–250.

Jensen, A. R. (1972). *Genetics and education.* New York: Harper & Row.

John, B., & Miklos, G. (1988). *The eukaryote genome in development and evolution.* Sydney: Allen & Unwin.

Jones, R. K., & Rubin, G. M. (1990). Molecular analysis of *no-on-transient A*, a gene required for normal vision in *Drosophila*. *Neuron, 4,* 711–723.

Joynson, R. B. (1989). *The Burt affair.* London: Routledge.

Kendler, K. S., & Robinette, C. D. (1983). Schizophrenia in the National Academy of Sciences – National Research Council twin registry: A 16 year update. *American Journal of Psychiatry, 140,* 1521–1563.

Konopka, R. J., & Benzer, S. (1971). Clock mutants of *Drosophila melanogaster*. *Proceedings of the National Academy of Sciences USA, 68,* 2112–2116.

Kulkarni, S. J., & Hall, J. C. (1987). Behavioral and cytogenetic analysis of the *cacophony* courtship song mutant and interacting genetic variants in *Drosophila melanogaster*. *Genetics, 115,* 461–475.

Kulkarni, S. J., Steinlauf, A. F., & Hall, J. C. (1988). The *dissonance* mutant of courtship song in *Drosophila melanogaster*: Isolation, behaviour and cytogenetics. *Genetics, 118,* 267–285.

Kyriacou, C. P. (1985). Long-term *ebony* polymorphisms: A comparison of the contributions of behavioral and non-behavioral fitness characters. *Behavior Genetics, 15,* 165–180.

Kyriacou, C. P. (1990). Genetic and molecular analysis of eukaryote behaviour. *Seminars in the Neurosciences*, *22*, 217–229.

Kyriacou, C. P. (1992). Sex variations. *Trends in Genetics*, *8*, 261–263.

Kyriacou, C. P., & Hall, J. C. (1986). Inter-specific genetic control of courtship song production and reception in *Drosophila*. *Science*, *232*, 494–497.

—— (1989). Spectral analysis of *Drosophila* courtship song rhythms. *Animal Behaviour*, *37*, 850–859.

—— (1993). Genetic and molecular analysis of *Drosophila* behaviour. *Advances in Genetics*, in press.

Kyriacou, C. P., Burnet, B., & Connolly, K. (1978). The behavioural basis of over-dominance in competitive mating success at the *ebony* locus of *Drosophila melanogaster*. *Animal Behaviour*, 26, 1195–1206.

Loehlin, J. C., Lindzey, G., & Spuhler, J. N. (1975). *Race differences in intelligence*. San Francisco, CA: Freeman.

Manning, A. (1961). The effects of artificial selection of mating speed in *Drosophila melanogaster*. *Animal Behaviour*, *9*, 82–91.

Nichols, R. C. (1978). Twin studies of ability, personality and interests. *Homo*, *29*, 158–173.

Plomin, R. (1988). The nature and nurture of cognitive abilities. In R. J. Sternberg (Ed.) *Advances in the psychology of human intelligence* (pp. 1–33). Hillsdale, NJ: Lawrence Erlbaum.

Plomin, R., & Defries, J. C. (1985). *Origins of individual differences in infancy: The Colorado Adoption Project*. New York: Academic Press.

Plomin, R., Defries, J. C., & Fulker, D. W. (1988). *Nature and nurture during infancy and early childhood*. New York: Cambridge University Press.

Plomin, R., Defries, J. C., & McClearn, G. E. (1990). *Behavioral genetics: A primer* (2nd edn). New York: Freeman.

Quinn, W. G., & Greenspan, R. J. (1984). Learning and courtship in *Drosphila*: Two stories with mutants. *Annual Review of the Neurosciences*, *21*, 67–93.

Rendahl, K. G., Jones, K. R., Kulkarni, S. J., Bagully, S. H., & Hall, J. C. (1992). The *dissonance* mutation at the *no-on-transient-A* locus of *Drosophila melanogaster*: Genetic conctrol of courtship song and visual behaviors by a protein with putative RNA-binding motifs. *Journal of Neuroscience*, *12*, 390–407.

Robertson M. (1989). False start on manic-depression. *Nature*, *342*, 222.

Scheller, R. J., & Axel, R. (1984). How genes control an innate behavior. *Scientific American*, *290*(3), 44–52.

Sherrington, R., Brynjolfsson, J., Petursson, J., Potter, M., Duddlestone, K., Baraclough, B. B., Wasmuth, J. J., Dobbs, M., & Gurling, H. M. D. (1988). Localization of a susceptibility locus for schizophrenia on chromosome 5. *Nature*, *336*, 164–167.

Tryon, R. C. (1940). Genetic differences in maze learning ability in rats. *National Society for the Study of Education 39th Yearbook*, *39*, 111–119.

Way, J. C. (1990). Determination of cell type in the nervous system. *Seminars in the Neurosciences*, *2*, 173–184.

Wender, P. H., Rosenthal, D., & Kety, S. S. (1968). A psychiatric assessment of the adoptive parents of schizophrenics. In D. Rosenthal & S. Kety (Eds) *The transmission of schizophrenia* (pp. 235–250). Oxford: Pergamon.

Wender, P. H., Rosenthal, D., Kety, S. S., Schulsinger, F., & Welner, J. (1974). Cross-fostering: A research strategy for clarifying the role of genetic and experimental factors in the etiology of schizophrenia. *Archives of General Psychiatry*, *30*, 121–128.

Wheeler, D. A., Kyriacou, C. P., Greenacre, M. L., Yu, Q., Rutila, J. E., Rosbash, M., & Hall, J. C. (1991). Molecular transfer of a species-specific courtship behaviour from *Drosophila simulans* to *Drosophila melanogaster*. *Science*, *251*, 1082–1085.

Wilson, R. S. (1983). The Louisville Twin Study: Developmental synchronies in behavior. *Child Development*, *54*, 298–316.

2

BEHAVIOURAL ECOLOGY AND EVOLUTION

John Lazarus

University of Newcastle upon Tyne, England

Theory in behavioural ecology
  Natural selection, fitness, and reproductive success
  Adaptation, optimization, and theoretical modelling
  Selection pressures
  Evolutionary stability and social behaviour
  The role of genetics
The scope of behavioural ecology
  Selfishness: why don't animals fight more fiercely?
  Cooperation: why should animals benefit others?
  Altruism: why should animals sacrifice themselves for others?
  Sex and parental care
    Competition for mates
    Mate choice
    Parental investment and mating strategies
Methods and prospects
Acknowledgement
Further reading
References

The aim of psychology is to understand the nature of behaviour and mental processes, and much of psychological endeavour is concerned with understanding causation; the conditions – social, environmental, physiological, or genetic – that are responsible for some behaviour, attitude, thought, or emotion. What environmental events cause an individual to behave aggressively, for example; what stimulates a male to court a female?

But for psychologists and biologists there is another kind of question, a "why?" kind of question. *Why* should certain events in the environment make an individual aggressive? Why, in general, do animals behave the way they do and not otherwise? Is there some common organizing principle that will provide an answer to all the disparate "Whys"?

There is such a principle: the process of evolution by *natural selection*. Species have evolved as a result of small accumulated changes in prior forms and, as a result of Darwin's (1859) insights, we know that the major force for such change has been the process of natural selection. The enormous importance of Darwin's theory is that it gives us a guiding principle for understanding the nature of life: the principle of *adaptation*. An adaptation is some feature of the animal's structure, physiology, or behaviour that solves some problem in its life. Darwin's theory of natural selection may not seem capable of predicting anything very profound or precise about behaviour but since the mid-1960s it has been enormously powerful in generating new theories to explain both the broad principles by which animals live their lives and the exquisite detail of their moment-to-moment decision-making. *Behavioural ecology* is the branch of psychology whose aim is to understand behaviour in terms of a history of evolutionary forces favouring adaptation.

THEORY IN BEHAVIOURAL ECOLOGY

Natural selection, fitness, and reproductive success

Darwin's (1859) theory of natural selection forms the starting-point for all further theorizing, and the logical structure of the theory is shown in Figure 1. Dawkins (1986) illuminates the theory brilliantly.

Natural selection predicts that phenotypic characters that increase *fitness*, compared to some alternative, will increase in frequency in the population. The fitness of an individual is a measure of its success at replicating itself in the next generation and can be measured as its *lifetime reproductive success* – the number of offspring it produces in its lifetime. A major aim of behavioural ecology is to test predictions about the way in which behaviour influences lifetime reproductive success.

As an example of the way in which natural selection moulds behaviour, imagine a gazelle that visits a waterhole to drink but in doing so runs some risk of predation by lions. How often will the gazelle go to drink if its behavioural decisions are the result of generations of natural selection acting on the decisions of its ancestors? We would expect the gazelle to make a trade-off between predation risk and the risk to its survival from dehydration (survival, to natural selection, being a means to the end of increasing reproductive success). An obvious prediction, therefore, is that drinking frequency will decline as the gazelle's perceived predation risk increases (e.g., as it detects lions more often by the waterhole) and increase as its water requirement becomes more pressing (for example, at higher temperatures). The gazelle's *optimal* decision – the precise drinking frequency that maximizes its survival chances as a result of both risks combined – can be predicted only

29

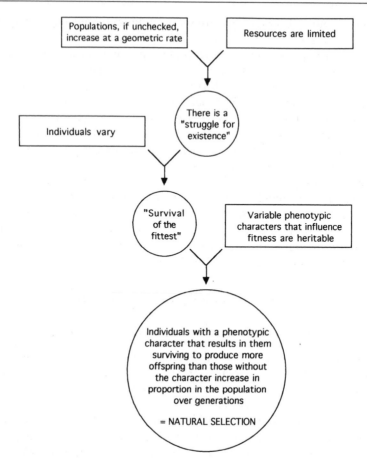

Figure 1   The structure of Darwin's (1859) theory of evolution by natural selection. Observations known to Darwin are shown in rectangles and Darwin's inferences in circles. A "phenotypic character" is simply some aspect of the individual's structure, physiology, or behaviour
Source: After Lazarus, 1987

if we know how the risk of death from predation and from dehydration are each influenced by drinking frequency. We would then have a *common currency* for the two conflicting consequences of drinking and would be able to calculate the rate of drinking that minimized the overall risk of death. An example where this is possible will be given later.

It is therefore possible to develop predictions about behaviour directly and simply from the theory of natural selection. This example also introduces the ubiquitous problem of *trade-offs*. In animal as in human life there are no free lunches and every investment in behaviour that brings some increase in fitness is accompanied by two kinds of disadvantage, or *fitness cost*. First, as in the gazelle's waterhole problem, the behaviour itself has costs as well as benefits; and second, there are always other, competing, demands on the individual's time that are being postponed. The drinking gazelle, for example, is taking valuable time out from feeding.

It is important to be clear about what is meant by an animal's "decisions" or "strategies". These terms describe choices made at the behavioural level and imply nothing about the cognitive processes involved, conscious or otherwise.

Adaptation, optimization, and theoretical modelling

Ideally, predictions in behavioural ecology would be made in terms of the influence of behaviour on lifetime reproductive success, and yet this is often difficult. For qualitative predictions of the kind "Waterhole visits will diminish as lion density increases", there is little problem. It can safely be assumed that more lions mean greater predation risk and that fewer waterhole visits will reduce that risk.

The problem comes with the more ambitious aim of testing whether animals have evolved optimal solutions to their problems, solutions that maximize fitness (Krebs & Kacelnik, 1991). If the effect of some behaviour on fitness cannot be measured, then we must look for some other consequence of behaviour that can be measured and that is assumed to be maximized when fitness is maximized.

For example, Parker (1978) developed a model to predict how long a male dung fly would copulate with a female on the assumption that he is selected to maximize the number of eggs fertilized per unit time. Parker found quite a good agreement between predicted and observed copulation time, which supports the hypothesis that natural selection has optimized copulation time in this species (Box 1). Note that the quantity assumed to be maximized here is not lifetime reproductive success but fertilization rate during some short period, and that the two quantities may not be optimized by the same behavioural option. This is because the short-term measure ignores costs borne later (e.g., predation risk while copulating), which influence the lifetime optimal value.

What should we conclude if the data did not fit the prediction? We could infer either that male copulation time is not optimized or that one or more of the model's assumptions are incorrect.

Box 1   The marginal value theorem and
           copulation time in the dung fly

Parker's (1978) model employs a theorem, the marginal value theorem (Charnov, 1976), which is used widely in behavioural ecology to predict how animals exploit resources, and gives a flavour of the optimality approach. It starts with the fact that resources (in this case females) are distributed patchily and that the male must travel from female to female in order to mate. While copulating he fertilizes eggs at a diminishing rate, as Parker discovered by interrupting copulating pairs at different times. When he moves to a new female he therefore swaps a low fertilization rate for a travel period with a zero rate followed by a period with a new female at an initially high rate.

When should he leave one female and seek out another in order to maximize fertilization rate? The solution is shown graphically in Figure 2. The rate of fertilization, taking into account both travel time and copulation time, can be drawn as a straight line on a graph of the number of eggs fertilized against time, starting with the onset of travel from the last female. The maximum fertilization rate is realized when this line just touches the diminishing returns curve of the number of eggs fertilized, and the optimal copulation time is the time at which this rate is achieved. The male is incapable of achieving a rate greater than this (a steeper line), and if the line was below this the male would have a lower fertilization rate than he was capable of achieving.

Parker's data and the predicted optimal copulation time are shown in Figure 2. The observed copulation time of 35.5 minutes is close to the predicted time of 41.4 minutes. Possible reasons for the discrepancy are discussed in the text.

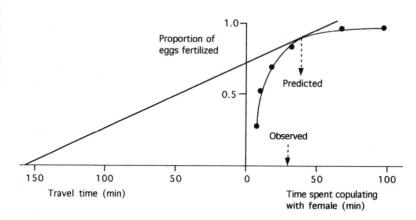

Figure 2 Predicting optimal copulation time in the male dung fly using the marginal value theorem. The average travel time between females (156.5 minutes) is shown to the left of the vertical axis, followed by the time spent copulating to the right of the vertical axis. When the male stops copulating the next cycle of travel and copulation begins

Source: Redrawn from Parker, 1978

How damaging would it be for the general belief in the adaptiveness of behaviour if we concluded that male copulation time was not optimal? First, optimality in copulation might have been compromised by a competing demand, such as hiding from predators. This would mean that the wrong criterion for optimality had been chosen, since it was the joint allocation of time devoted to copulation and hiding that had been selected, just as we expected the gazelle's waterhole problem to be solved in terms of two conflicting demands. A study demonstrating adaptive trade-offs between gathering resources and avoiding predation is described in Box 2.

Second, there might be some *constraint* that prevents an optimal solution

---

Box 2   Measuring a feeding-predation trade-off
in a common currency: patch choice in an ant species

Animals of many species will choose a food patch giving a lower rate of food intake if by doing so they avoid a predation risk, thereby demonstrating their ability to trade-off conflicting demands in an adaptive manner. The study coming closest to measuring such conflicting demands in a common fitness currency is that by Nonacs and Dill (1990) on the ant *Lasius pallitarsis*.

In this elegant study ants were given the choice of foraging from two sites with liquid diets differing in concentration, and therefore in the volume of nutrient that could be carried back to the colony by each ant worker on each foraging trip. The path from the colony to the more concentrated solution sometimes contained a larger predatory ant and a worker had a 1 in 57 chance of being killed if it chose this path.

The common currency employed for the consequences of food gathering and predation risk was the growth in mass of the colony. Foraging increased growth by the production of new eggs and the growth of larvae, while predation reduced growth by loss of worker adults. While eggs, larvae, and adults may not be exactly equivalent in terms of colony fitness, fast colony growth is certainly important for survival and reproduction.

Ants tended to forage from the patch that gave the greater net colony growth, taking into account both egg and larval gains and adult losses. More impressively, risky and safe patches were valued equally when a colony growth of 0.98 mg was balanced by the loss of one worker, weighing on average 1.37 mg. Given a range of worker weights of 0.90–2.20 mg and the fact that worker size is not too important for the job of gathering liquid food, workers have done impressively well at the job of maximizing colony growth.

---

being reached (Krebs & Kacelnik, 1991). In the present example it might be a constraint on the ability of the male to control the behaviour of the female. Finally, the behaviour might be sub-optimal for two reasons even though there are no constraints or competing demands. First, environmental factors influencing the optimum might have changed too recently or be fluctuating too fast to have been tracked by selection. Second, the behaviour may be correlated with another trait, more important for fitness, whose optimal value does not coexist with that of the behaviour in question (Price & Langen, 1992).

As Darwin (1872) himself made clear, natural selection does not predict optimization, but only that the option most enhancing fitness, of those available in the population, will come to predominate:

> Natural selection tends only to make each organic being as perfect as, or slightly more perfect than, the other inhabitants of the same country with which it comes into competition. . . . Natural selection will not produce absolute perfection, nor do we always meet, as far as we can judge, with this high standard under nature. (p. 163)

The merit of optimization models, however, is that they provide precise and testable predictions and a sensible starting-point for the investigation of adaptation; there is no sense in developing a model that predicts, say, 90 per cent of an optimal value. Where they fail, a study of the possibilities outlined above leads to a fuller understanding. Quite often, however, such models are vindicated by the data, often enough for us to realize now that animals have a quite astonishing ability to achieve optimal solutions to complex problems.

Selection pressures

A selection pressure is a feature of the animal's environment that influences fitness by acting on features of its phenotype. For the gazelle at the waterhole, for example, predation is a selection pressure on its drinking behaviour. A selection pressure can itself be an adaptation. For example, the mating strategy of male red deer is to defend a number of females from other males in a harem, but this is possible only because females congregate on the best swards to graze. Food dispersion and predation are selection pressures on female congregation which, in turn, is a selection pressure on the male's mating strategy (Emlen & Oring, 1977). Feeding efficiency and predator avoidance are ubiquitous selection pressures on behaviour.

Evolutionary stability and social behaviour

The optimal value for, say, the time to be spent grazing by a goose will be influenced by many factors, but is unlikely to be affected by the grazing times of other geese. Social behaviour, however, is different in an important way.

The fitness consequences of a social act depend on the response it receives, and its fate under natural selection therefore depends on the relative frequency with which it encounters different responses. Selection is then said to be *frequency-dependent*.

Imagine, for example, two strategies for competing over resources. The first is to fight for it viciously, the second to threaten the opponent but to withdraw if things get nasty. If most of the population threaten, a rare fighter will do well since it beats every threatener it meets, and most of its opponents are threateners. Natural selection therefore favours fighters and they increase in frequency. As they do so, however, they meet each other more often as opponents and now lose some encounters, often sustaining injury. The success of fighting therefore depends on its frequency in the population. What will be the outcome? Will fighters take over the entire population or will they wipe each other out, leaving only the more peaceful threateners? Could both strategies coexist in the population at stable frequencies, or might the evolutionary outcome be an endless cycle of fluctuating frequencies? The answer to this particular problem is given later, but more generally we wish to know if there is a *stable* outcome to the evolutionary history of some social action and, if so, what it will be.

A stable set of strategies may not achieve their greatest fitness (i.e., be optimal) at stability and yet it is stable frequencies that we expect to find in nature since, by definition, these are the ones that endure. Natural selection therefore tends to produce stable behavioural strategies and not necessarily optimal ones. Maynard Smith (1976a) developed these ideas first in the context of competitive behaviour and coined the term *evolutionarily stable strategy* (ESS) for the strategy observed in the stable state. The concept of evolutionary stability is now seen to be fundamental to an understanding of the evolution of social behaviour, and is arguably the most important contribution to the study of behavioural evolution since Darwin's theory of natural selection (Maynard Smith, 1982).

The role of genetics

The evolution of behaviour by natural selection requires that behaviour is heritable but not that it is fully determined by genes. In fact much behavioural variability is a result of animals responding adaptively to variations in the environment. What is inherited by the fitter individuals is then a set of learning rules that produces more adaptive responses to environmental input. For example, ants make adaptive patch choices as a result of nutrient and predation risk experiences on the patches (Box 2).

THE SCOPE OF BEHAVIOURAL ECOLOGY

A major division in the subject matter of behavioural ecology is that between social and non-social behaviour, study of the former being termed *sociobiology*.

Acquisition of resources, such as food, is an animal's most pressing non-social problem (although it becomes a social problem if individuals compete or cooperate in gathering resources). One approach to studying optimality in resource acquisition has been exemplified by the male dung fly's copulation time problem (Box 1), which is treated as a non-social problem since the female is assumed to take a passive role. This area is reviewed by Krebs & Kacelnik (1991).

Social behaviour influencing survival can be classified in terms of the *benefits* and *costs* to the fitness of the actor and recipient of the social act (Hamilton, 1964), where benefit means an increase in fitness and cost a decrease. Figure 3 illustrates the four possible outcomes defined in this way. The terms used there are familiar in the context of human motivation, but in behavioural ecology they are defined solely in terms of the consequences of action for fitness and imply nothing about motives or emotions. Spite, in which neither party benefits, is at best a rare occurrence in the animal world (Lazarus, 1987).

In discussing social behaviour I shall concentrate on some major problems that remained unsolved until the development since the 1960s of new theories that have revolutionized our understanding of behavioural evolution.

Selfishness: why don't animals fight more fiercely?

Since natural selection favours competitive success, the evolution of selfishness is not difficult to understand. The problem is not to understand why animals are competitive but why they are not more so; why aggressive disputes are not more injurious and why they often involve merely display. The large carnivores, for example, refrain from attacking each other in the way they treat their prey. The answer briefly is that hawkish tactics of all-out

	Receiver	
	Benefit	Cost
Actor Benefit	Cooperation	Selfishness
Actor Cost	Altruism	Spite

Figure 3 Four categories of social behaviour defined in terms of the consequence for fitness to actor and receiver. Benefit = increase in fitness; cost = decrease in fitness

attack carry a risk of injury and are therefore often unstable, as Maynard Smith (1976a) demonstrated. The essence of the argument, and of the method employed, can be appreciated by considering the very simplest of his models.

Imagine two strategies for competition over a resource, "Hawk" and "Dove" (Maynard Smith, 1976a) – like the fighter and threatener described above – which involve three tactics: display, escalate (with a risk of injury), and retreat. A Hawk always escalates a fight until either it is injured, and loses, or its opponent retreats. A Dove displays but if its opponent escalates it retreats before getting injured. When two Hawks meet each is equally likely to win the resource, which increases fitness by an amount V, whereas injury reduces it by W. Similarly, when two Doves compete each is equally likely to win after a period of display which costs them both T units of fitness due to the time and energy involved.

To analyse the evolutionary outcome Maynard Smith (1976a) employed the methods of game theory, which already had a long history of application to human social interaction. The average change in fitness (or "payoff") to Hawk and Dove of fighting each type of opponent is cast in a *payoff matrix* as shown in Figure 4. For example, when a Hawk meets another Hawk it wins (payoff $= V$) and loses (payoff $= -W$) with equal probability, giving a mean payoff of $(V - W)/2$. When a Dove meets another Dove it is equally likely to win $(V - T)$ or lose $(-T)$, resulting in a mean payoff of $(V/2) - T$. We now seek an evolutionarily stable strategy, or ESS; that is, a strategy which, if adopted by most members of the population, has a greater payoff than any other strategy in the game.

We examine the case where $W > V$, since we are interested in the fate of hawkish behaviour, which is greater when $W > V$ than when the reverse is true. With this scenario a Hawk mutant arising in a population of Doves would have a payoff of V (Figure 4) while Doves gain only $((V/2) - T)$ in fights against each other. Since $V > ((V/2) - T)$ selection favours Hawks, which will therefore increase in frequency over generations. In the same way

When competing against

		HAWK	DOVE
Payoff to	HAWK	$(V - W)/2$	V
	DOVE	0	$(V/2) - T$

Figure 4 Payoff matrix for the competitive game between Hawks and Doves

a Dove mutant in a population of Hawks fares better than the dominant strategy, since $0 > (V - W)/2$. This means that the stable outcome is a mixture of Hawks and Doves – a *mixed ESS* – at frequencies which give the two strategies equal payoff. This simple model shows that all-out attack is not necessarily favoured by natural selection because of the injuries sustained when most individuals are hawkish.

Since this pioneering use of game theory, more realistic models have been developed incorporating real-life differences between individuals. For example, individuals differ in their ability to win an encounter as a function of their size and strength and may use reliable indicators of strength to assess their chances of winning an escalated contest, the weaker animal withdrawing before it risks injury. Common toads assess each other's size by listening to the depth of their opponents' croaks, since large males reliably produce deeper croaks (Davies & Halliday, 1978).

Cooperation: why should animals benefit others?

Why should an individual behave so as to increase the fitness of another, even if it benefits in the process itself? It is not difficult to think of cases where cooperation is obviously adaptive. Wolves hunting together in a coordinated pack, for example, can bring down a large animal like a moose, a task almost impossible for a single animal. However, a more subtle problem remains. Why don't animals that receive the fruits of cooperation without reciprocating replace those that give as well as receive?

The answer to this problem was provided by Axelrod and Hamilton (1981) and their solution shows once more the importance of ESS thinking. If individuals meet only once, then selection will favour a selfish strategy which "defects" on the system of cooperation. However, if individuals meet repeatedly, and can modify their behaviour as a function of past experience, then more subtle strategies can develop in which defectors can be penalized. Axelrod and Hamilton found that a simple strategy, TIT FOR TAT, was an ESS in competition against many others, provided that the probability of individuals meeting again was sufficiently high. TIT FOR TAT cooperates on the first encounter and then does on every subsequent encounter whatever its opponent did on the previous encounter. It is therefore a strategy of cooperation based on reciprocity. Several examples of reciprocity have now been studied in detail, including the sharing of blood by vampire bats.

Altruism: why should animals sacrifice themselves for others?

The suicidal sting of the honeybee; the sharing of food by lions; the alarm call that warns others but attracts the attention of a predator: how can natural selection explain such behaviour when its mechanism is based on selfish competition, the very antithesis of altruism (Figure 3)?

Until the 1960s it was commonly believed that natural selection could act at the level of the group or species. In this climate Wynne-Edwards (1962) argued that altruism would be selected if it aided population survival by preventing overexploitation of resources. He made the analogy of the advantage of setting fishing limits to maintain fish stocks for the long-term benefit of all fishing fleets.

The problem with this argument is that a selfish individual in a group of altruists would have a greater reproductive success, so that selfishness would be favoured by selection and spread through the population (Maynard Smith, 1976b). The evolutionary origins of altruism must therefore be sought at the level of the individual or in some cases, as we shall see, at the level of the gene (Dawkins, 1989).

One origin for altruism is as a component of cooperation. When the mutual benefit of cooperation is realized by the reciprocation of altruistic acts (Trivers, 1971) then each altruistic act is explicable in the wider context of Axelrod and Hamilton's (1981) theory of cooperation described above.

To appreciate the second major way in which altruism might evolve we must abandon the Darwinian notion of the individual as the unit of selection. Whilst selection pressures act directly on the individual's phenotype, the heritable unit responsible for changes in phenotype frequencies over time is the gene (Dawkins, 1989).

A special property of social behaviour is that it affects the fitness not only of the performer but also of the recipient of the social act. Now, if the recipient bears the same genes that influenced the act in the performer, the evolutionary fate of the behaviour in question will be determined by its consequences for the fitness of both parties, since both bear the relevant genetic material. The behaviour pattern will be favoured by natural selection as long as it results in the genes controlling it having a greater chance of replication into the next generation. It follows that the unit upon which natural selection acts is, most generally, the gene rather than the individual.

The benefit arising from altruistic behaviour relies on the beneficiary of the altruism bearing the altruistic gene. The commonest way in which individuals come to share the same genes is by inheriting them by recent common descent. A parental gene, for example, has a probability of .5 (i.e., a 50–50 chance) of appearing in one of its offspring, and full siblings have the same chance of sharing a gene by common descent from a parent. This probability is termed the *coefficient of relatedness*, r.

Now, suppose an altruistic act produces a cost C to the actor and a benefit B to the recipient, to which it is related by r. The genes promoting altruism will be benefited if the relative contains them, which it does with probability r. So, on average, the benefit of such acts to the relevant genes is equal to Br. For natural selection to favour the altruistic act its benefit must outweigh its cost, so that the condition favouring altruism between relatives can be expressed as $Br > C$. For altruism between full sibs ($r = .5$) to be favoured, for example, the benefit must be greater than twice the cost.

This gene-centred view, and the condition derived from it above for the evolution of altruism (Hamilton, 1964), has necessitated a new measure to replace the Darwinian concept of individual fitness. Hamilton introduced the concept of *inclusive fitness*, which takes into account the effects of social acts directed towards and received from relatives, and Maynard Smith coined the term *kin selection* to describe the action of natural selection on interactions between relatives. Since altruism between relatives is common in nature these ideas have thrown light on a great variety of social actions, from parental care to alarm calls and from cooperative breeding in birds and mammals (Emlen, 1991) to the ultimate altruism of the worker castes of ants, bees and wasps which forgo reproduction to raise their sisters (Box 2).

Sex and parental care

In moving from the analysis of social strategies of survival to those of reproduction and parental care we encounter a far more complex set of problems. In the first place, sexual and parental strategies generally involve more than a single interaction. Individuals may form relationships with sexual partners for one or more breeding episodes in order to raise offspring, so that long-term strategies of exploitation and cooperation become possible. Long-term strategies also characterize the parent–offspring relationship (Clutton-Brock, 1991; Trivers, 1974).

Second, we need to understand the evolution of two sets of interdependent strategies, male and female. This means a search for three ESSs, each of which depends on the outcome of the other two: one for males, one for females, and one for the combination of male and female strategies. This is a formidable task with much still to be achieved. At present we understand the major evolutionary forces determining sexual and parental strategies, and some of the variation in these strategies across the animal kingdom in terms of the costs and benefits to the individuals involved. In addition, quantitative studies have revealed the detailed workings of selection on particular aspects of sexual and parental behaviour in a number of species (e.g., Davies, 1992).

Understanding the different reproductive strategies of males and females starts with a simple principle. An individual can enhance its reproductive success by increasing the number of offspring that it brings into the world and by improving the survival chances of each offspring. This starting-point leads us to predict the existence of competition for mates and mate choice: a preference for mates that produce more or fitter offspring (Lazarus, 1987). Mate choice, in turn, favours advertisement of the attributes of favoured sexual partners. The evolutionary forces favouring mate competition and mate choice are termed, respectively, *intra-sexual* and *inter-sexual selection*.

Competition for mates and mate choice are ubiquitous in nature but are sexually biased, males commonly competing for females and females exercising a choice between males. Why are the sex roles generally arranged in this way?

Competition for mates

These questions are matters of current debate but the first major contribution was made by Trivers (1972), a century after Darwin's (1871) pioneering work on sexual selection. Trivers showed the central importance of parental care for the evolution of sexual strategies and his argument stems from the fundamental difference between the sexes. Males are defined as the sex producing a large number of small gametes − sperms − while females produce a small number of large gametes − eggs. The gamete is the first act of *parental investment* (PI) that a parent makes in its offspring, PI being defined as any act by a parent that increases the fitness of its offspring at the cost of the parent's ability to produce other offspring (Trivers, 1972).

The sex difference in gamete size means that a male's initial PI in his offspring is less than the female's. Since an offspring is less costly for a male to produce it follows that the male's optimal number of offspring, and therefore his optimal number of matings, is greater than the female's (Trivers, 1972). With the usual 1 : 1 sex ratio, and the rapid rate at which sperm can be renewed compared to eggs, competition between males for access to females is therefore inevitable. Consequently, intra-sexual selection favours greater size and strength in males, and the evolution of weapons such as the antlers of male deer. In the primates, for example, sexual dimorphism in body size increases with the number of females per male in a breeding group (Figure 5; Clutton-Brock, Harvey, & Rudder, 1977). Where this sex ratio is higher males can increase their reproductive success to a greater extent by competing successfully for females with other males, so this relationship can be understood as the result of intra-sexual selection. It is also an example of the *comparative method*, by which cross-species comparisons provide evidence relating to adaptive hypotheses (Harvey & Pagel, 1991).

Males have also evolved methods of *sperm competition*, designed to prevent the sperm of competitors from reaching a female's eggs. Insects flush out the sperm of other males from the female with their penis before inseminating her, or cement up her genital opening after copulation. Male birds copulate with their mates more frequently if they are likely to have mated recently with another male (Birkhead & Møller, 1991). Another strategy is to guard the female from other males. The male dung fly, for example, guards the female between copulation and egg laying to prevent his sperm being removed by a later male, and this guarding period is part of the "travel time" involved in his optimal copulation time problem (Box 1).

Clutton-Brock and Vincent (1991) argue that competition is determined by the relative rates of reproduction of the two sexes. The sex that completes its

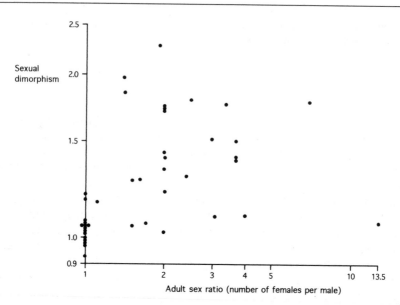

Figure 5 The degree of sexual dimorphism (male weight/female weight) increases with the average number of females per male in a breeding group across 42 primate species. Each point is a different species
Source: Redrawn from Clutton-Brock, Harvey, and Rudder, 1977

parental duties and is free to breed again more quickly will, on average, have more members in the breeding population, whose *operational sex ratio* (Emlen & Oring, 1977) will thus be biased towards that sex. The majority sex will therefore compete for the sex in the minority, which becomes a *limiting resource* for the majority sex.

Where females bear the major parental burden, as in mammals, we therefore expect males to be the sexually competing sex, as is the case. While in mammals the arguments based on relative PI and relative reproductive rates therefore make the same prediction, mating patterns in fish are more satisfactorily explained in terms of reproductive rates. In many fish species the male cares for the developing eggs and yet males still compete for females. This is partly because males are able to guard batches of eggs at the same time as courting females, so that parental duties do not limit their time in the breeding population (Gross & Sargent, 1985).

Mate choice

The exertion of some choice on the part of the female seems a law almost as general as the eagerness of the male. (Darwin, 1871)

Delilah was a floosy...
She wasn't choosy.
(Ira Gershwin)

Female choice of male partners also follows from the above arguments based on sex differences in PI and reproductive rates. If males attempt to mate with more than one female, or if the operational sex ratio is male biased, then females will be courted by a number of males and have the opportunity to choose between them. Darwin (1871) did not explain the evolution of female preferences, but later theorists have shown how preference for a male trait, and the trait itself, can coevolve to produce exaggerated male characters like the peacock's tail. This has been a controversial issue, involving the idea that a preferred male trait must "handicap" the male in order to indicate his true fitness to a female (reviewed by Maynard Smith, 1991). Females may select males for the resources they can give the young or for traits of high fitness their offspring will inherit.

Parental investment and mating strategies

The sex difference in gamete size can explain sex differences in competition and mate choice where there is no further parental investment in the young. However, as Trivers (1972) argued, it is the sex difference in *total* PI that influences mating strategies. A parent will be selected to continue investing in its offspring as long as the net benefit (i.e., benefit minus cost) of this option exceeds that of deserting the young and seeking new breeding opportunities elsewhere (Clutton-Brock, 1991). This is a complex problem since the consequences of desertion for offspring survival may depend crucially on whether the other parent also deserts, so that desertion decisions will be selected to take into account the desertion decisions of the partner. Once again, ESS analysis and game theory are the analytical tools for tackling this problem (Lazarus, 1990; Maynard Smith, 1977).

However, the broad taxonomic variation in parental care and mating patterns can be understood as coevolved adaptations following the rules outlined above. Compare, for example, the commonest patterns shown by birds and mammals. The majority of bird species are monogamous, with males competing for the superior breeding territories preferred by females (Vehrencamp & Bradbury, 1984). The male commonly helps his mate to care for the eggs and young although he has the opportunity to desert her after copulation. Male care is probably favoured because of the importance of parental feeding for offspring survival, a view supported by the greater incidence of male care in species with altricial young, which require feeding in the nest, compared to those with precocial young (such as ducklings) which are able to feed for themselves soon after hatching. Furthermore, experimental removal of the male in a number of altricial species reduces offspring fitness (Clutton-Brock, 1991).

In mammals, female lactation frees the male from the requirement of feeding the young and consequently male care and monogamy are rare in this group, polygyny and promiscuity being the common mating systems.

This kind of cost-benefit analysis does not provide the whole answer, however, since male strategies of PI may be constrained as a result of female choice. If females reject a male who is already mated, because of the disadvantage of sharing his parental duties with another female, then monogamy may be imposed on males. However, a female may accept an already mated male if he can offer her sufficient resources to compensate for the disadvantage of sharing (Vehrencamp and Bradbury, 1984).

METHODS AND PROSPECTS

As we have seen, behavioural ecologists generate predictions by verbal arguments and mathematical models based on the theory of natural selection. Predictions are tested by observations and experiments that relate behaviour to environmental influences and its consequences for some component of the individual's fitness. Alternatively, predictions can be tested by comparing the adaptations of different species operating under different selection pressures and constraints (e.g., Figure 5). Such comparisons represent natural experiments offered by the evolutionary process (Harvey & Pagel, 1991).

Exciting new insights are offered by DNA fingerprinting, a technique that allows the relatedness between individuals to be determined with confidence. It is showing, for example, that males of supposedly monogamous species like the house sparrow are sneaking off to sire offspring on neighbouring territories.

These methods are demonstrating how far adaptive decision making penetrates into all aspects of an animal's life.

ACKNOWLEDGEMENT

I am grateful to Stuart Laws for preparing the figures.

FURTHER READING

Dawkins, R. (1989). *The selfish gene* (2nd edn). Oxford: Oxford University Press.
Krebs, J. R., & Davies, N. B. (1987). *An introduction to behavioural ecology* (2nd edn). Oxford: Basil Blackwell.

REFERENCES

Axelrod, R., & Hamilton, W. D. (1981). The evolution of cooperation. *Science, 211,* 1390–1396.

Birkhead, T. R., & Møller, A. P. (1991). *Sperm competition in birds.* London: Academic Press.

Charnov, E. L. (1976). Optimal foraging: The marginal value theorem. *Theoretical Population Biology, 9,* 129–136.

Clutton-Brock, T. H. (1991). *The evolution of parental care.* Princeton, NJ: Princeton University Press.

Clutton-Brock, T. H., & Vincent, A. C. J. (1991). Sexual selection and the potential reproductive rates of males and females. *Nature, London, 351,* 58–60.

Clutton-Brock, T. H., Harvey, P. H., & Rudder, B. (1977). Sexual dimorphism, socionomic sex ratio and body weight in primates. *Nature, London, 269,* 797–800.

Darwin, C. (1859). *The origin of species by means of natural selection, or the preservation of favoured races in the struggle for life* (1st edn). London: John Murray.

Darwin, C. (1871). *The descent of man, and selection in relation to sex.* London: John Murray.

Darwin, C. (1872). *The origin of species by means of natural selection, or the preservation of favoured races in the struggle for life* (6th edn). London: John Murray.

Davies, N. B. (1992). *Dunnock behaviour and social evolution.* Oxford: Oxford University Press.

Davies, N. B., & Halliday, T. R. (1978). Deep croaks and fighting assessment in toads *Bufo bufo. Nature, London, 274,* 683–685.

Dawkins, R. (1986). *The blind watchmaker.* Harlow: Longman.

Dawkins, R. (1989). *The selfish gene* (2nd edn). Oxford: Oxford University Press.

Emlen, S. T. (1991). Evolution of cooperative breeding in birds and mammals. In J. R. Krebs & N. B. Davies (Eds) *Behavioural ecology: An evolutionary approach* (3rd edn, pp. 301–337). Oxford: Basil Blackwell.

Emlen, S. T., & Oring, L. W. (1977). Ecology, sexual selection and the evolution of mating systems. *Science, 197,* 215–223.

Gross, M. R., & Sargent, R. C. (1985). The evolution of male and female parental care in fishes. *American Zoologist, 25,* 807–822.

Hamilton, W. D. (1964). The genetical evolution of social behaviour, I and II. *Journal of Theoretical Biology, 7,* 1–16, 17–52.

Harvey, P. H., & Pagel, M. D. (1991). *The comparative method in evolutionary biology.* Oxford: Oxford University Press.

Krebs, J. R., & Kacelnik, A. (1991). Decision-making. In J. R. Krebs & N. B. Davies (Eds) *Behavioural ecology: An evolutionary approach* (3rd edn, pp. 105–136). Oxford: Basil Blackwell.

Lazarus, J. (1987). The concepts of sociobiology. In H. Beloff & A. M. Colman (Eds) *Psychology survey 6* (pp. 192–217). Leicester: British Psychological Society.

Lazarus, J. (1990). The logic of mate desertion. *Animal Behaviour, 39,* 672–684.

Maynard Smith, J. (1976a). Evolution and the theory of games. *American Scientist, 64,* 41–45.

Maynard Smith, J. (1976b). Group selection. *Quarterly Review of Biology, 51,* 277–283.

Maynard Smith, J. (1977). Parental investment: A prospective analysis. *Animal Behaviour, 25,* 1–9.

Maynard Smith, J. (1982). *Evolution and the theory of games.* Cambridge: Cambridge University Press.

45

Maynard Smith, J. (1991). Theories of sexual selection. *Trends in Ecology and Evolution*, *6*, 146–151.

Nonacs, P., & Dill, L. M. (1990). Mortality risk vs. food quality trade-offs in a common currency: Ant patch preferences. *Ecology*, *71*, 1886–1892.

Parker, G. A. (1978). Searching for mates. In J. R. Krebs & N. B. Davies (Eds) *Behavioural ecology: An evolutionary approach* (1st edn, pp. 214–244). Oxford: Basil Blackwell.

Price, T., & Langen, T. (1992). Evolution of correlated characters. *Trends in Ecology and Evolution*, *7*, 307–310.

Trivers, R. (1971). The evolution of reciprocal altruism. *Quarterly Review of Biology*, *46*, 35–57.

Trivers, R. (1972). Parental investment and sexual selection. In B. Campbell (Ed.) *Sexual selection and the descent of man 1871–1971* (pp. 136–179). Chicago, IL: Aldine.

Trivers, R. (1974). Parent–offspring conflict. *American Zoologist*, *14*, 249–264.

Vehrencamp, S. L., & Bradbury, J. W. (1984). Mating systems and ecology. In J. R. Krebs & N. B. Davies (Eds) *Behavioural ecology: An evolutionary approach* (2nd edn, pp. 251–278). Oxford: Basil Blackwell.

Wynne-Edwards, V. C. (1962). *Animal dispersion in relation to social behaviour*. Edinburgh: Oliver & Boyd.

3

THE NERVOUS SYSTEM AND THE BRAIN

Daniel Kimble

University of Oregon, USA

The human nervous system consists of the brain, spinal cord, and peripheral nervous system, and is composed of many billions of cells. There are two distinctive cell types in the nervous system, *neurons* and *neuroglial* cells. Neurons, of which there are estimated to be at least 10^{11} in the human brain, are specialized to process, transmit, and store information. These functions depend on two basic attributes of neurons, their capacity to generate and conduct electrical signals and their ability to manufacture, secrete, and respond to a variety of chemical substances. It is estimated that there are several times as many neuroglial (glial) cells as neurons in the nervous system. Although glial cells do not produce nerve impulses, they are essential to the proper operation of the nervous system. Different types of glial cells are known to serve to (1) provide structural support and possibly guidance for migrating neurons during embryonic development; (2) produce the insulating myelin sheath around the axons of many neurons; and (3) remove debris and secrete neurotrophic factors following injury to the nervous system. It is axiomatic among modern researchers that all of our observable behaviour, as well as all of our thoughts, emotions, and dreams − in short, all mental life − is generated by activity of neurons and glial cells in the nervous system.

STRUCTURE AND FUNCTION OF NEURONS

Neurons come in a variety of shapes and sizes, but (with rare exceptions) they all share certain morphological features. The neuronal cell body contains the nucleus, which in turn contains the genetic material of the cell. Outside the nucleus in the cytoplasm of the cell can be found cellular components necessary for the synthesis of proteins. It is instructive to realize that once differentiated, neurons in mammals do not again undergo mitosis (cell division). Thus, many neurons in long-lived species survive for many decades. Glial cells, on the other hand, retain the capacity to undergo mitosis, as do most other cell types in the body. In vertebrates, processes (branches) from the neuronal cell termed *dendrites* serve as important sites for synaptic contacts from other neurons, as does the cell body itself. Some synapses are also found on axon terminals. On some neurons in the cerebral cortex and hippocampus, dendrites are studded with *dendritic spines*. These spines are common sites for synapses. The shape and number of spines are abnormal in some neurological conditions, and have been demonstrated to increase in number in enriched environments in laboratory rats (Greenough, 1975). The *axon* is the output segment of the neuron. Axons also emerge from the cell body, often branch several times, forming *axon collaterals*, and form specialized *axon terminals* which make contact with postsynaptic cells, either other neurons, muscle cells, or gland cells.

In order to understand the ability of the neuron to conduct electrical signals, it is necessary to consider the structure of the cell membrane. The neuronal cell membrane is similar to other animal cell membranes in many ways, but with significant specializations. Neuronal membranes are composed of a *lipid* bilayer to which are attached sugars, proteins, and glycoproteins. It is the particular mix of proteins that define different functional regions of the cell membrane.

Electrical signalling by neurons

An electrical potential of 60–70 millivolts occurs across the neuronal membrane, caused by a slightly unequal distribution of *ions* (charged particles produced by the dissociation of substances in the watery medium of the brain). In all cases known, the interior of the neuron is negative with respect to the outer surface of the membrane. The basic form of communication in the nervous system is by means of electrical signals generated and conducted by neurons. These signals in turn cause the release of chemical neurotransmitter substances as the electrical signal invades the axon terminals. Two basic classes of electrical signals can be recorded in the nervous system: *nerve impulses*, occurring primarily in the axon of the sending neuron, and *postsynaptic potentials*, produced primarily in the dendrites and cell body of the receiving neuron. Postsynaptic potentials can be either excitatory or inhibitory, while nerve impulses are excitatory only.

Four ion species are involved in producing these electric signals: sodium, potassium, chloride, and calcium. Sodium, potassium, and calcium are all positively charged ions (*cations*), while chloride carries a negative charge and is termed an *anion*. Modern understanding of the role of ion movements underlying electric signalling in neurons stems from the pioneering research of Andrew Hodgkin and Alan Huxley at Cambridge University in the 1950s and 1960s (Hodgkin, 1964; Hodgkin & Huxley, 1952). Although precise details vary among different neurons, it appears universally true that the movement of sodium ions from the outer surface of the cell membrane to the interior of the neuron is responsible for initiating a nerve impulse. The movement of potassium ions from the interior of the cell to the outer surface of the membrane underlies the restoration of the original resting potential, setting the stage for subsequent nerve impulses. Ion movement takes place through specialized *ion channels*, usually, but not always, specific for a particular ion species. Ion channels regulate the flow of ions across the neuronal membrane by changing their shape slightly in response to voltage changes across the membrane, the presence of specific chemical neurotransmitters, or both. In the axon the movement of ions through ion channels is regulated by the moment-to-moment voltage across the membrane. At synapses located in the dendrites and cell body, the presence of neurotransmitters regulates ion movement.

Sodium and potassium also participate in postsynaptic potentials. Whether the resulting potential is inhibitory or excitatory depends on the direction of movement of these cations. Outward movement of cations (e.g., potassium) is inhibitory, moving the potential across the membrane further away from the point where a nerve impulse can be produced (termed a *hyperpolarizing event*). Inward movement of cations (e.g., sodium), is excitatory for the opposite reason, and is termed a *depolarizing event*. Chloride is primarily involved in inhibitory postsynaptic potentials by moving inward, hyperpolarizing the membrane.

Calcium is involved in a multitude of cellular functions. For example, the release of chemical neurotransmitter by a nerve impulse is calcium dependent. Calcium ions are also involved in many cellular responses to neurotransmitters. In many of these processes, a *second messenger system* is activated by the binding of a neurotransmitter to specialized receptors located on the external surface of the neuronal membrane. Several different second messenger systems are known to be present in the nervous system. The richness of the responses to various neurotransmitters available to the neuron makes the neuron an extremely flexible information signalling device.

Once initiated, nerve impulses travel down the axon toward the axon terminals where neurotransmitter release occurs. The conduction speed of a nerve impulse depends on the diameter of the axon and the degree to which it is myelinated (covered in a fatty sheath). Larger axons and heavy myelination both increase conduction speed. In warm-blooded animals, axonal conduction rates vary from less than 1 m/sec to over 100 m/sec.

Synapses

The invasion of the axon terminals by the nerve impulse initiates a series of events at the *synapse*. A synapse is a junction between neurons, consisting of the *presynaptic* axon terminal, a small gap or *synaptic cleft* that separates the cells involved, and a *postsynaptic* receptive region. Both electrical and chemical synapses are known to exist in vertebrates. At electrical synapses, the presynaptic neuron passes on the nerve impulse to the postsynaptic neuron through specialized ion channels in the two cells that line up directly across from one another, allowing for passage of ionic current with little loss of signal strength. Chemical synapses are more common in the brains of vertebrates than electrical synapses, and have attracted most of the research efforts since 1920. Chemical neurotransmitters are stored in *synaptic vesicles* in the axon terminals, and are released as the nerve impulse invades the axon terminals. Calcium ions are directly responsible for neurotransmitter release. The depolarization caused by the nerve impulse opens ion channels located in the axon terminals. Calcium ions then enter the terminal and cause the release of the neurotransmitter (Llinas, 1982). Neurotransmitter molecules then diffuse across the synaptic cleft and interact with specific *synaptic receptor molecules* located in the membrane of the postsynaptic neuron. This results either in the direct change in shape of ion channels (as in the case of the neurotransmitter acetylcholine) or, more commonly, in the activation of one or more second messenger systems within the postsynaptic cell. One of the main results of second messenger activation is also a change in ion channel shape. Thus, either directly or indirectly, neurotransmitters influence ion movement across the postsynaptic membrane by altering the shape of the proteins that form the ion channels. The resultant *postsynaptic potentials* can be either excitatory or inhibitory, depending on the identity of the ion channels involved. Although both nerve impulses and postsynaptic potentials are caused by ionic currents across the membrane, they are quite different in several respects. Table 1 lists some of these differences.

Whether or not the combined effect of the postsynaptic potentials on a

Table 1 Comparison of nerve impulses and postsynaptic potentials

	Nerve impulses	*Postsynaptic potentials*
Amplitude	Approximately 110 mV	< 1 mV to 15–20 mV
Direction	Always depolarizing	Either hyperpolarizing or depolarizing
Duration	1–10 msec	Up to several minutes
Propagation	Without decrement	With decrement
Ion channels	Voltage regulated sodium and potassium	Chemically regulated sodium potassium, chloride

given neuron results in a change in the rate of production of nerve impulses in that neuron depends on the moment to moment algebraic summing of depolarizing and hyperpolarizing events in that neuron. Such activity is constantly occurring in the nervous system. If sufficient depolarization is produced, an increase in the firing rate will occur in the postsynaptic neuron. If hyperpolarization dominates, the postsynaptic cell will be silenced or will reduce its firing rate. An individual neuron may make as many as 100,000 or more synaptic contacts with other neurons.

The current list of neurotransmitters is certain to be incomplete, as new candidates are added to the list from time to time. Strong evidence exists for at least ten neurotransmitters. These include *acetylcholine* and biogenic amines such as *noradrenaline (norepinephrine)*, *adrenalin (epinephrine)*, *dopamine, serotonin*, and *histamine*. Another group includes some amino acids and their derivatives such as *gamma-amino butyric acid (GABA)*, *glutamate, glycine*, and *aspartate*. There appear to be two or more different varieties of receptors for each neurotransmitter. The variety of available neurotransmitters and receptors provides the nervous system with remarkable flexibility of action.

FUNCTIONAL NEUROANATOMY

Historical perspective

Knowledge of the structure of the nervous system has accumulated over centuries. An early authority was Galen (AD 129–199), a physician, who placed great importance on the cavities in the brain (what we know now as the *ventricles*), rather than the brain itself. Galen suggested that these cavities contained the fluids or "spirits" that governed our actions. The legacy of these erroneous ideas lingered into the nineteenth century. The first known drawings of the human brain made directly from cadavers are found in *De Humani Corporis Fabrica*, which was written by the Flemish anatomist Andreas Vesalius (1514–1564), and published in 1543. Although gradual

51

progress was made between the sixteenth and nineteenth centuries, it was not until the end of the nineteenth century that substantial knowledge about the structure of neurons and glial cells was available. Two individuals can be singled out in this regard, Italian anatomist Camillo Golgi (1843–1926), and Spanish anatomist Santiago Ramón y Cajal (1852–1934). These two shared the Nobel Prize for medicine in 1906. Ironically, Ramón y Cajal, using a staining procedure developed by Golgi, demonstrated beyond doubt that the nervous system is composed of individual cells and is not a reticulum or network of connected elements as Golgi had proposed. The development of the electron microscope in the middle of the twentieth century, along with other technical advances, ushered in the modern period of neuroanatomy, which remains an extremely active and changing field.

Divisions of the nervous system

The nervous system can be divided into two connected parts, the central nervous system (CNS), consisting of the brain and spinal cord, and the peripheral nervous system (PNS), composed of the cranial and spinal nerves and the autonomic nervous system (ANS) (Figure 1). Over 99 per cent of all neurons and glial cells are in the CNS. Nevertheless, the PNS contains elements vital to normal functioning. For example, all of the nerves that convey sensory impressions from the skin and many sense organs belong to the peripheral nervous system (the sensory neurons in the retina of the eye, however, belong to the central nervous system). The axons of the motor nerves that innervate the muscles of the body are also part of the PNS. Also, the autonomic nervous system that innervates various internal organs and whose activity is prominent in emotional responses is an element of the PNS. The ANS in turn is composed of two distinct divisions, the sympathetic

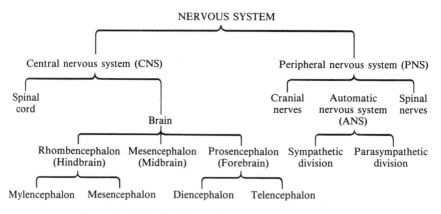

Figure 1 Main divisions of the human nervous system

division, whose activity accompanies emergency, energy expending situations ("fight or flight"), and the parasympathetic division.

Functions of the autonomic nervous system

In general, parasympathetic activity tends to produce results that oppose those of the sympathetic division; thus the parasympathetic division is more active during energy conserving times, as when we rest or digest food. Thus, sympathetic activity increases the rate and force with which the heart beats, while parasympathetic activity does the opposite. No simple generalization can cover all of the activities of the ANS, however, and both divisions are known to work together in some cases. For example, both erection and ejaculation are crucial for successful reproduction by male vertebrates. The changes in blood flow required for erection are regulated by nerves belonging to the parasympathetic division, while ejaculation is controlled by nerves from the sympathetic division. These two divisions must thus operate in a coordinated sequence.

Cranial and spinal nerves

The remainder of the PNS in humans is made up of 12 pairs of cranial nerves and 31 pairs of spinal nerves. The cranial nerves, designated by Roman numerals, are listed in Table 2, along with their main functions. The spinal nerves innervate skeletal muscles (those attached to bones, as opposed to smooth muscles such as in the gut), mediating both sensation and motor control via separate neuronal pathways. Spinal nerves are named for the region of the vertebral column from which they emerge; thus there are eight pairs of cervical nerves, twelve pairs of thoracic nerves, five pairs of lumbar

Table 2 Cranial nerves

	Nerve	*Main functions*
I	Olfactory	Perception of odours
II	Optic	Vision
III	Oculomotor	Regulation of eye movements
IV	Trochlear	Regulation of eye movements
V	Trigeminal	Face sensations; chewing
VI	Abducens	Regulation of eye movements
VII	Facial	Taste sensations; face movements
VIII	Auditory	Hearing; equilibrium
IX	Glossopharyngeal	Taste sensations; swallowing
X	Vagus	Internal organ sensation and control
XI	Accessory	Vocal cord; neck movements
XII	Hypoglossal	Tongue movements

nerves, five pairs of sacral nerves, and one pair of coccygeal nerves. As determined in the nineteenth century by Charles Bell (1774–1842) in England, and François Magendie (1783–1855) in France, each spinal nerve has two divisions, or roots. The dorsal (rear) root contains sensory neurons from the skin, joint, and muscles, while the ventral (front) root contains the axons of motor neurons which activate the muscles. This early discovery, known as *the law of roots*, encouraged workers at the time to seek other specializations in the nervous system. Sensory pathways that carry nerve impulses from the periphery to the CNS are also known as *afferent*, while *efferent* neurons, such as the motor neurons in the ventral root, carry nerve impulses from the CNS to the periphery. The terms afferent and efferent are also used with respect to neurons entering and leaving various areas of the brain and spinal cord.

Divisions of the brain

The human brain has evolved into the most complex living organ in the known universe, and our knowledge of its structure and function is, naturally, incomplete. Nevertheless, some consistent findings have emerged from basic research that comes from the examination of patients from the neurological clinic, from laboratory work with animals, and other sources.

The basic divisions of the human brain start to form during the first five weeks of fetal life, when the neural tube changes its shape to form five bulbous enlargements which are recognized as the basic divisions of the brain. Early in development, the most posterior division is the *rhombencephalon* or *hindbrain* (*cephalon* means "head"). The rhombencephalon further divides to form the *myelencephalon* and the *metencephalon*. The middle of the five divisions is the *mesencephalon* or *midbrain*. The most anterior enlargement is the *prosencephalon*, or *forebrain*. About the fifth week of gestation this divides to form the final two divisions, the *diencephalon* and the *telencephalon*. These five divisions plus the spinal cord provide a meaningful organization for the vertebrate nervous system (see Figure 1).

The entire CNS, brain and spinal cord, is surrounded by a covering of three membranes or *meninges*. The outermost of these is the *dura mater*, a tough, fibrous sheet of cells. The innermost layer, directly in contact with the underlying tissue is the thin, delicate, transparent *pia mater*. In between the pia mater and the dura mater is the *arachnoid layer*. Between the dura mater and the pia mater is the subarachnoid space, filled with cerebrospinal fluid (CSF), secreted by specialized cells in the ventricles. The meninges and CSF protect the brain, cushioning it to some extent from blows to the skull.

Hindbrain structures

Several notable regions of the brain are located in the hindbrain. These are the *medulla oblongata*, and the *pons* (see Figure 2). The medulla oblongata forms a core within the hindbrain, while the pons ("bridge") is the name given to the ventral and anterior portion of the hindbrain. Both the medulla oblongata and the pons contain ascending and descending nerve tracts as well as nuclei (clusters of neuronal cell bodies with associated glia) serving both motor and sensory functions. Several cranial nerves enter and leave the hindbrain. The pons is involved in processes of sleep and dreaming. It contains cholinergic neurons which are thought to help usher in rapid eye movement (REM) sleep, a periodic phase of sleep proven in humans to correlate highly with reports of dreaming. Injections of acetylcholine into the pons reliably produce REM sleep in experimental animals (Hobson, 1988).

Another major brain component develops from the dorsal surface of the hindbrain, the *cerebellum* ("little brain"). The cerebellum is critically involved in many functions including the modification and guidance of co-ordinated movements, and the maintenance of postural balance and muscle tone. There are two features of the cerebellum worth noting. First, it operates

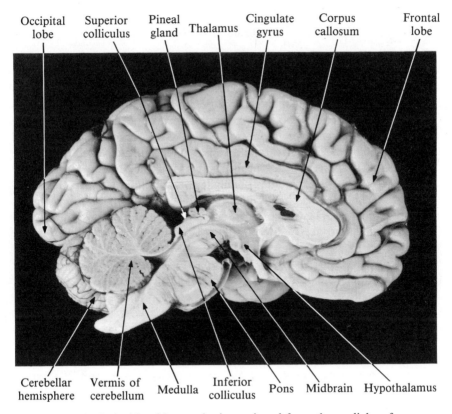

| Occipital lobe | Superior colliculus | Pineal gland | Thalamus | Cingulate gyrus | Corpus callosum | Frontal lobe |

| Cerebellar hemisphere | Vermis of cerebellum | Medulla | Inferior colliculus | Pons | Midbrain | Hypothalamus |

Figure 2 Left side of human brain as viewed from the medial surface

without intruding on our consciousness. For example, patients with cerebellar damage may stumble and fall, but they do not feel dizzy. Similarly, input from various sensory systems (vision, equilibrium, etc.) enters the cerebellum but does not produce any conscious awareness such as is generated by input into the sensory regions of the cerebral cortex. Second, the cerebellum is believed to act indirectly to carry out its functions. Output from the cerebellum, carried by *Purkinje* neurons, does not go to motor neurons directly, but to other intermediate components of the motor system, such as those in the brain stem and cerebral cortex.

Beginning in the hindbrain and extending well into the midbrain is the *reticular formation*, a network ("reticulum") of neurons thought to be critical for regulating levels of consciousness and attention through their influence on forebrain structures such as the cerebral cortex and hippocampus. Damage to the reticular formation, as can occur with tumours or severe blows to the head, can produce coma and even death. Neurons in this system are involved in the production of different stages of consciousness such as sleep and waking.

Midbrain structures

The hindbrain merges into the midbrain at the anterior end of the pons. The dorsal surface of the midbrain is marked by two structures, the *inferior* and *superior colliculi* ("little hills", singular *colliculus*). There is an inferior colliculus and a superior colliculus on each side of the midline. The superior colliculi are composed of two regions, a superficial and a deeper part. The superficial region receives input from neurons of the optic nerve, visual regions of the cerebral cortex and a region of the frontal lobes termed the *frontal eye fields*. The superficial layers are concerned with orienting responses to visual stimuli, but probably play no significant role in image formation. The deeper layers of the superior colliculi do not receive input directly from the optic nerve, but do receive input from several different brain regions. The deeper layers seem to be concerned with orienting to stimuli in various modalities (Wurtz & Albano, 1980). The inferior colliculi are part of the auditory pathway and relay information originating in the ear to the medial geniculate nucleus in the thalamus.

The internal core of the midbrain contains portions of the reticular formation, including the *locus ceruleus* ("blue place"). This important nucleus contains about 20,000 neurons in humans, and axons go from the locus ceruleus throughout the forebrain, innervating virtually all regions of the cerebral cortex and hippocampus. The widespread influence of these nuclei (there is one on each side of the brain) has attracted considerable theoretical interest in the role of the locus ceruleus in control of waking and sleeping, forebrain arousal and attentional mechanisms. The main neurotransmitter found in neurons originating in the locus ceruleus is noradrenalin.

56

Other important structures in the midbrain include a series of midbrain nuclei, the *raphe* ("seam") nuclei and the *substantia nigra* ("black substance"). Raphe neurons secrete *serotonin* as their major neurotransmitter, while those of the *substantia nigra* use *dopamine*. The raphe nuclei are, like the locus ceruleus, concerned with regulation of states of waking and sleeping, while the substantia nigra is part of the motor control system. The raphe nuclei are located along the midline. Degeneration of neurons in the substantia nigra is found in *Parkinson's disease*, a condition characterized by involuntary tremors of the limbs and torso, profound slowness in initiating and performing movements, and a shuffling walk. As is true of the hindbrain, the midbrain also contains many ascending and descending nerve tracts, as well as various nuclei involved in a variety of functions. For example, the *central grey* is the name given to a series of nuclei located at the centre of the midbrain. These neurons are known to be involved in the reception and modulation of pain sensations.

Forebrain structures

During development the forebrain forms two structures, the *diencephalon* and the *telencephalon*. The diencephalon is the more caudal of these two. These are the most recently evolved parts of the brain, and contain those regions thought to be most directly involved in higher mental functions such as perception, thinking, language, etc. It should be kept in mind, however, that without the normal functioning of the phylogenetically older parts of the brain, such as the reticular formation, these so-called "higher" structures cannot operate normally. Although some localization of function may be possible within the brain, the interaction of systems located throughout the brain and spinal cord are necessary for the production of all but the simplest of reflex behaviours. Nevertheless, the size of the cerebral cortex in humans, other primates, and some other mammals such as the cetaceans attests to the fundamental importance of this and other forebrain structures in the emergence of sophisticated mental operations seen in these species.

The junction of midbrain and the diencephalon in humans is marked on the dorsal surface of the brain by the *pineal gland*. This tiny, unpaired organ has attracted attention since the time of René Descartes (1596–1650), who suggested that the pineal gland was the location within the brain where mind and body interacted. Its function remains obscure in humans, although it is known that this gland participates in the control of annual reproductive cycles in hamsters and in the regulation of daily activity-rest rhythms in some species of birds. There is speculation that the pineal gland in humans may influence the timing of puberty and also play a role in *seasonal affective disorder* (SAD), a form of depression linked to the short day length.

The *thalamus* ("room") and the *hypothalamus* ("below the room") comprise two major regions of the diencephalon. These are major components of the brain and house nuclei involved in many different functions. The thalamus, for example, contains neurons that participate in the processing of information from each of the different senses (except that of olfaction). Thus, the *lateral geniculate nucleus* receives input from the optic nerve and sends and receives messages to and from regions of the cerebral cortex involved in vision. The *medial geniculate* nucleus performs similar functions within the auditory system. Other nuclei are concerned with other senses. Some nuclei in the thalamus participate in *non-specific* (not related to any specific sensory system) input that reaches the cerebral cortex from the reticular formation. The hypothalamus, located just below the thalamus, contains a rich variety of nuclei and nerve tracts involved in many diverse activities such as eating, drinking, temperature regulation, reproductive functions, and timing of various rhythmic activities in the body. Also, the hypothalamus contains *neurosecretory neurons* that release *hypothalamic hormones* into a specialized, local blood system that carries these hormones directly to the *anterior pituitary gland* attached to the base of the hypothalamus. Hypothalamic hormones regulate the synthesis and release of hormones from the anterior pituitary. The hormones released from the anterior pituitary in turn travel in the general blood supply to influence other organs in the body such as the gonads and adrenal glands. This arrangement means that mental and emotional events can directly influence the hormonal system via hypothalamic hormones. Also, hormones secreted by the gonads, adrenal glands, and other *endocrine* organs can penetrate to the brain and influence neural circuits and thus affect behaviour, mood, and thoughts, as well as further release of hypothalamic hormones.

Another important group of structures in the forebrain are the *basal ganglia*; this group includes the *caudate* ("comet") *nucleus*, the *globus pallidus* ("pale globe"), and the *putamen* ("peachstone"). The basal ganglia are known to be involved in the initiation and execution of movements, although it is probable that these structures are also active in many other functions as well. Axons from substantia nigra neurons to the basal ganglia degenerate in Parkinson's disease, while in *Huntington's chorea* neurons in the basal ganglia itself degenerate.

Another loosely associated group of brain structures are identified as the *limbic* ("border") *system*, named by the French physician Paul Broca (1824–1880), who observed that these structures tend to form a border or ring around the medial face of the cerebral hemisphere (Nauta & Feirtag, 1986). Structures generally included in the limbic system include the *hippocampus* ("seahorse"), *amygdala* ("almond"), *septal nuclei*, and *cingulate* ("belt") gyrus (see Figure 3). The limbic system has been a focus for research for many years, and a number of theories have been proposed regarding limbic system function. The hippocampus is known to be an important component in a medial temporal lobe memory system that participates in the processing of memories of events in an individual's life. Damage to the hippocampus in humans, such as occurs as an aftermath of some viral brain infections produces a profound *anterograde amnesia* (loss of memory for events occurring after the damage), and considerable *retrograde amnesia* (loss of memory for prior events) as well.

Functions of the amygdala, septal nuclei, and cingulate gyrus are poorly understood, but it is likely that all, particularly the amygdala, play some role in the attachment of emotional significance to various stimuli. Removal of the temporal lobes, including the amygdala (a cluster of several different

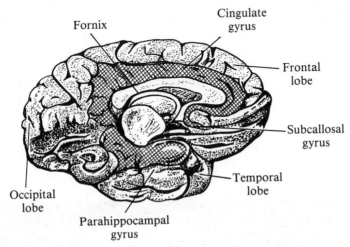

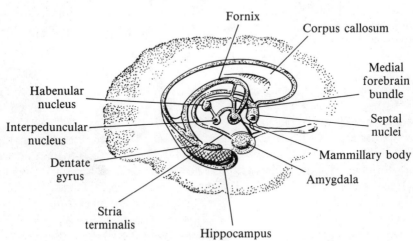

Figure 3 Limbic system structures. *Upper left*: Medial view of left hemisphere, showing cingulate gyrus, parahippocampal gyrus, and fornix. *Lower right*: View of limbic system structures not visible from the medial surface: hippocampus, dentate gyrus, amygdala, septal nuclei, and mammillary body

nuclei buried in the tip of the temporal lobe) is known to produce dramatic changes in the emotionality of monkeys. The constellation of symptoms produced by bilateral temporal lobe removal is known as the Klüver-Bucy syndrome after the workers who first noted these changes in the 1930s (Klüver & Bucy, 1939). Although rare, this syndrome has also been noted in humans following bilateral temporal lobe damage.

Cerebral cortex

The most impressive evolutionary advance in mammalian brains is seen in the dramatic increase in the size and complexity of the cerebral cortex. Nowhere is this more evident than in the primate order, particularly in humans. A progression index developed to assign numbers to the degree of evolution of different brain regions (Stephan, 1972) accords the human cerebral cortex a score of 156. The cerebral cortex of the chimpanzee, our nearest existing relative, receives a 60. The human hippocampus, by contrast, scores 17, and the cerebellum 4. As can be seen in Figure 4, the cerebral cortex entirely covers the rest of the brain of the two cerebral hemispheres. The cortex of primates and several other mammals is so greatly enlarged that it folds in on itself, forming the characteristic ridges or *gyri*, and fissures or *sulci*. Containing

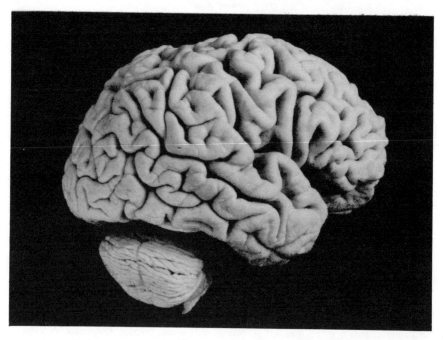

Figure 4 Human brain as seen from posterior aspect, showing gyri and sulci

over 10^{10} neurons, and perhaps five to ten times that many glia cells, the cerebral cortex is a multi-layered sheet of cells some 2.5–4 mm in thickness. By convention, six layers of cells and their processes can be distinguished, although most schemes also identify several sub-layers (see Figure 5). Because of its appearance in fresh brain tissue, the cortex itself is called *grey matter*, while the underlying layer of axons covered with myelin is termed *white matter*.

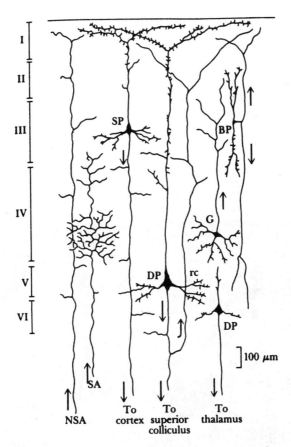

Figure 5 Neuronal cell types in cerebral cortex. Drawing based on Golgi stained cells. Abbreviations: NSA = non-specific afferent; SA = specific afferent; SP = superficial pyramidal cell; DP = deep pyramidal cell; BP = bipolar cell; G = granule cell; rc = recurrent collateral axon branches. Roman numerals at left refer to layers of the cortex

Cell types in the cortex

Although neurons in the cerebral cortex display many different shapes, a useful classification divides cortical neurons into one of two categories — pyramidal and non-pyramidal or stellate cells (Peters & Jones, 1984). Figure 6 shows these cell types as revealed by Golgi staining. The pyramidal neurons are widely viewed as the primary output or "executive" neurons in the cortex. Although originally named because of the shape of the cell body, some pyramidal cells actually have spherical or ovoid cell body shapes. Pyramidal cells are generally oriented perpendicular to the surface of the brain, and characterized by a single large apical dendrite which extends vertically from the top or apex of the cell body and several basal dendrites which extend from the base of the cell body in a horizontal fashion. These dendrites, particularly the apical dendrites, are usually studded with hundreds of dendritic spines. Dendritic spines are suspected of being one of the main places where brain changes underlying learning happen (e.g., Baudry & Lynch, 1987; Kandel, 1991a, 1991b). The axon of pyramidal cells typically emerges from the base of the cell body and usually (but not always) joins the underlying white

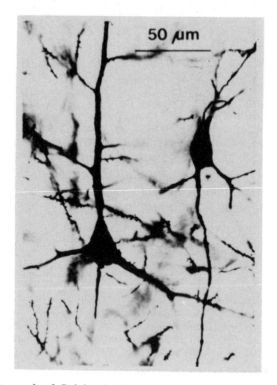

Figure 6 Photograph of Golgi stained pyramidal neuron (lower left), and stellate cell (upper right)

matter and projects to other regions of the brain. These projections can be to the opposite hemisphere of the brain, via the large interconnecting band, the *corpus callosum*, or other interhemispheric nerve tracts such as the anterior and posterior commissures. Other pyramidal cells project to subcortical areas, or to other regions of the same hemisphere. Some pyramidal neurons project several centimetres to synapse with motor neurons in the spinal cord.

A wide variety of neurons fall into the non-pyramidal or stellate cell category. Non-pyramidal cells lack the prominent apical dendrite. A variety of cell body shapes, dendritic branches and axonal ramification have been noted for these cells. While pyramidal neurons can send axons long distances in the brain and are therefore viewed as output neurons from the cortex, most non-pyramidal neurons have axons that branch and synapse in a much more localized fashion, and generally do not leave the region where their parent cell body is found. Thus, it is assumed that non-pyramidal neurons primarily perform local circuit duties within the cortex.

Functional columns in the cortex

Considerable evidence suggests that much of the cerebral cortex is organized into *functional columns* of neurons which, within a given column, all share some closely related function. For example, it is known that in the visual cortex of cats and monkeys vertical columns exist that respond primarily to impulses from one eye or the other (*ocular dominance columns*), while still other columns contain neurons that respond primarily to lines or edges with narrowly defined orientations (*orientation columns*) (Hubel & Wiesel, 1979). In the somatosensory cortex, columns with similar response properties have also been identified. These vertically oriented columns have been suggested to form the basic neural modules that underlie functional organization throughout widespread regions of the cortex (Mountcastle, 1979). The size of these columns varies from 30 to 500 micrometres (millionths of a metre) in diameter, and contain from a few hundred to a few thousand neurons. These columns were originally determined by recording the responses of individual neurons while presenting various stimuli to the animal. In recent years, various anatomical techniques have confirmed the existence of these columns.

Architectonic maps of the cortex

In the early part of the twentieth century, various neuroanatomists proposed different maps of the cerebral cortex based on their observations of regional differences in cell structure as seen with the light microscope. Most of these *architectonic maps* are of historical interest only, but the one produced by Korbinian Brodmann in 1909 continues to be used by modern workers, and

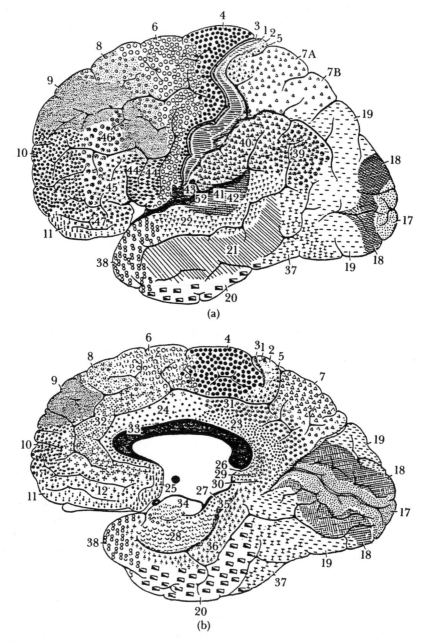

Figure 7 Brodmann numbering system for various architectonic areas of human cortex

Brodmann numbers still serve as useful referents to various regions of the human brain (see Figure 7).

Functional regions of the cortex

Our knowledge of functional distinctions among various regions of the cortex has accumulated gradually over the past 150 years. In fact, many brain researchers, perhaps put off by the eccentric claims of localization of function proposed by phrenologists such as Gall and Spurzheim in the nineteenth century, rejected the idea of localization of function until well into the twentieth century. More recently, however, the evidence for functional modules, albeit often involving dispersed circuits in the cortex, is now compelling. The first major evidence for localization of function in the human brain was Broca's discovery in 1861 that severe *aphasia* (loss of language function) was associated with damage to the posterior region of the *left* frontal lobe. This discovery not only provided an impetus for further thinking about localization of function but also, for the first time, suggested that the right and left cerebral hemispheres of human beings were not identical in function. As Broca put it, "*Nous parlons avec l'hémisphère gauche!*" ("We speak with the left hemisphere!") (Kandel, 1977, p. 10). Over a century was to pass before it was recognized that the right and left cerebral hemispheres were not structural mirror images either (Geschwind & Levitsky, 1968). In particular, a structure in the temporal lobe of humans known as the *planum temporale* (temporal plane) is larger in the left hemisphere in about 71 per cent of human brains, larger in the right in about 15 per cent of cases, and about the same size in 14 per cent (Witelson, 1983). Other anatomical asymmetries have also been observed, although their functional significance remains uncertain (Kolb & Whishaw, 1990).

Information concerning possible functional differences between the left and right cerebral hemispheres in humans has come from study of neurological patients with unilateral brain damage, neurosurgical patients, and studies of normal subjects using brain imaging techniques such as *positron emission tomography* (PET scanning). In addition, one notable series of experiments has been performed on epileptic patients who have had the major intercerebral commissures surgically cut to stop the spread of seizure activity from one hemisphere to the other. Such surgery allows an experimenter to present visual and tactile stimuli to each hemisphere independently, taking advantages of the anatomical organization of the sensory pathways involved. These experiments, conducted by Roger Sperry and his colleagues (e.g., Gazzaniga & Le Doux, 1978; Sperry, 1968; 1982) have shown that under laboratory conditions, each hemisphere can display "two independent streams of conscious awareness, one in each hemisphere" (Sperry, 1968). Such patients have also reinforced the view that the left hemisphere is, in most individuals, specialized to mediate language *production*, while the right hemisphere tends to be superior in various pattern perception skills such as recognition of faces and visual patterns that cannot be easily given a verbal label. Controversy exists concerning the capacity of the minor (usually right) hemisphere to *comprehend* language, although there is agreement that it is considerably more limited than is that of the dominant hemisphere.

Modern brain imaging techniques such as positron emission tomography have opened new research possibilities for exploring localization of function in the conscious human brain. For example, PET scans of subjects responding to verbal stimuli have shown those specific areas of the brain that are more active as subjects perform different language related tasks. These studies are forcing the revision of theories of brain organization dating back to the nineteenth century (Petersen, Fox, Posner, Mintun, & Raichle, 1988). Prospects for understanding the functions of the human brain have never been brighter.

FURTHER READING

Adelman, G. (Ed.) (1987). *Encyclopedia of neuroscience* (2 vols). Boston, MA: Birkhäuser.

Kandel, E. R., Schwartz, J. H., & Jessell, T. M. (Eds) (1991). *Principles of neural science* (3rd edn). New York: Elsevier.

Kimble, D. P. (1992). *Biological psychology* (2nd edn). Orlando, FL: Harcourt Brace Jovanovich.

Kolb, B., & Whishaw, I. Q. (1990). *Fundamentals of human neuropsychology* (3rd edn). New York: Freeman.

Nauta, W. J. H., & Feirtag, M. (1986) *Fundamental neuroanatomy*. New York: Freeman.

REFERENCES

Baudry, M., & Lynch, G. (1987). Properties and substrates of mammalian memory systems. In H. Y. Meltzer (Ed.) *Psychopharmacology: The third generation of progress* (pp. 449–462). New York: Raven.

Gazzaniga, M. S., & Le Doux, J. E. (1978). *The integrated mind*. New York: Plenum.

Geschwind, N., & Levitsky, W. (1968). Human brain: Left–right asymmetries in temporal speech region. *Science, 161*, 186–187.

Greenough, W. T. (1975). Experiential modification of the developing brain. *American Scientist, 63*, 37–46.

Hobson, J. A. (1988). *The dreaming brain*. New York: Basic Books.

Hodgkin, A. L. (1964). *The conduction of the nerve impulse*. Liverpool: Liverpool University Press.

Hodgkin, A. L., & Huxley, A. F. (1952). A quantitative description of membrane current and its application to conduction and excitation in nerves. *Journal of Physiology, 117*, 500–544.

Hubel, D. H., & Wiesel, T. N. (1979). Brain mechanisms of vision. *Scientific American, 241*, 150–162.

Kandel, E. R. (Ed.) (1977). *Handbook of physiology: A critical, comprehensive presentation of physiological knowledge and concepts* (2nd edn, sectn 1, vol. 1). Bethesda, MD: American Physiological Society.

Kandel, E. R. (1991a). Brain and behavior. In E. R. Kandel, J. H. Schwartz, & T. M. Jessell (Eds) *Principles of neural science* (3rd edn, pp. 5–17). New York: Elsevier.

Kandel, E. R. (1991b). Cellular mechanisms of learning and the biological basis of individuality. In E. R. Kandel, J. H. Schwartz, & T. M. Jessell (Eds) *Principles of neural science* (3rd edn, pp. 1009–1030). New York: Elsevier.

Klüver, H., & Bucy, P. C. (1939). Preliminary analysis of functions of the temporal lobe in monkeys. *Archives of Neurology and Psychiatry, 42*, 979–1000.

Kolb, B., & Whishaw, I. Q. (1990). *Fundamentals of human neuropsychology* (3rd edn). New York: Freeman.

Llinas, R. R. (1982). Calcium in synaptic transmission. *Scientific American, 247*, 38–47.

Mountcastle, V. B. (1979). An organizing principle for cerebral function: The unit module and the distributed system. In F. O. Schmitt & F. G. Worden (Eds) *The neuroscience fourth study program* (pp. 21–41). Cambridge, MA: Massachusetts Institute of Technology Press.

Nauta, W. J. H., & Feirtag, M. (1986). *Fundamental neuroanatomy.* New York: Freeman.

Peters, A., & Jones, E. G. (1984). Classification of cortical neurons. In A. Peters & E. G. Jones (Eds) *The cerebral cortex: vol. 1. Cellular components of the cerebral cortex* (pp. 107–121). New York: Plenum.

Petersen, S. E., Fox, P. T., Posner, M. I., Mintun, M., & Raichle, M. E. (1988). Positron emission tomographic studies of the cortical anatomy of single-word processing. *Nature, 331*, 585–589.

Sperry, R. W. (1968). Hemispheric deconnection and unity in conscious awareness. *American Psychologist, 23*, 723–733.

Sperry, R. W. (1982). Some effects of disconnecting the cerebral hemispheres. *Science, 217*, 1223–1226.

Stephan, H. (1972). Evolution of primate brains: A comparative anatomical investigation. In T. Tuttle (Ed.) *The functional and evolutionary biology of primates* (pp. 155–174). Chicago, IL: Aldine-Atherton.

Witelson, S. F. (1983). Bumps on the brain: Right–left anatomic asymmetry as a key to functional lateralization. In S. J. Segalowitz (Ed.) *Language functions and brain organization* (pp. 117–144). New York: Academic Press.

Wurtz, R. H., & Albano, J. E. (1980). Visual-motor function of the primate superior colliculus. *Annual Review of Neuroscience, 3*, 189–226.

4

SLEEP AND DREAMING

J. Allan Hobson

Harvard Medical School, Massachusetts, USA

With its increasing emphasis upon functional questions, sleep research has entered a new and exciting third phase. Since sleep had never been objectively studied in any detail prior to the beginning of its first phase in about 1950, it was to be expected that much of the early work in the field would be descriptive. (For reviews of the early work, see Jouvet, 1972; Moruzzi, 1972.) Sleep proved a more complex behaviour than such distinguished physiologists as Pavlov (1960) and Sherrington (1955) had imagined, and, even in the 1990s, new discoveries continue to be made, especially in the clinical realm. In the second phase of sleep research, beginning about 1960, specific mechanistic theories began to be enunciated and tested. New cellular and molecular research techniques produced a spate of findings that have gained conceptual and empirical coherence (Hobson, Lydic, & Baghdoyan, 1986; Hobson, 1988; Steriade and Hobson, 1976). While incomplete, the mechanistic approach is still going strong, promising to inform – and be informed by – the third phase research on sleep function that has recently been initiated (see reviews, Hobson, 1988, 1989).

Sleep is regarded as an evolutionarily recent, emergent, and "higher" function of the brain. In its fully developed form in humans – a cycle of dreamless Non-Rapid Eye Movement (NREM) sleep followed by Rapid Eye Movement sleep accompanied by dreaming – sleep is clearly a complex function; yet, even in unicellular organisms or single cells, sleeplike behaviour is present, organized differentially over time in sequential phases of rest and activity responsiveness and unresponsiveness (Aschoff, 1965a; Moore-Ede, Czeisler, & Richardson, 1983). The circadian rhythm (of about one day in length) is the best-known example of the temporal organization of physiological functions, but rhythms with shorter (infradian) and longer (ultradian) periods are now widely recognized. Thus, it would seem that the rhythm of rest and activity (the primordia of sleeping and waking) is one of the most universal and basic features of life.

While rest states are seen in all organisms, sleep as we define and measure it in warm-blooded mammals has many significant features not seen in lower animals. Thus, although the reptiles and birds have both high-voltage and low-frequency electroencephalogram (EEG) patterns and diminished responsiveness (as in mammalian NREM sleep), they evince no REM phase despite having all the brain-stem structures used by mammals to activate their brains periodically in sleep. The only exceptions are birds, who show brief REM episodes in the first few days after hatching. They lose this sleep state as they mature, thus paralleling the dramatic decline in sleep – and especially REM – that occurs in the early development of all young mammals (Roffwarg, Muzio, & Dement 1966). Amphibians have none of the sleep features of mammals and, unless their temperature falls, they remain constantly alert even when immobile and relaxed for long periods of time.

I begin this chapter by defining the states of waking, NREM, and REM sleep and their behavioural, electrographic, and psychological activity changes that allow for the investigation of the functional implications of sleep and dreaming. I shall then describe the most recent findings regarding the functional roles of the different states of the brain-mind, not only because they are exciting in their novelty, but also because they strongly support some of our common-sense notions about the importance of sleep. Whatever ultimately stands as the truth of the matter, it is already clear that sleep is a global organismic phenomenon, and its study can integrate in an illuminating way many domains of behavioural and psychological science with neurobiology.

SLEEP

Behavioural and psychological definition of sleep

Sleep is a behavioural state of homeothermic (warm-blooded) vertebrate mammals defined by characteristic changes in posture; raised sensory thresholds; and distinctive electrographic signs. Sleep is usually associated with a marked diminution of motor activity and with the assumption of recumbent postures. Typically the eyes close and the somatic musculature becomes relaxed. As sleep deepens, threshold to external stimulation increases and animals become progressively more unresponsive to external stimuli (see Figure 1).

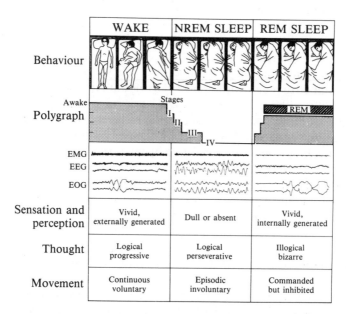

Figure 1 Behavioural states in humans. The states of waking, NREM, and REM sleep have behavioural, polygraphic, and psychological manifestations which are depicted here. In the behavioural channel, posture shifts – detectable by timelapse photography or video – can be seen to occur during waking and in concert with phase changes of the sleep cycle. Two different mechanisms account for sleep immobility: disfacilitation (during states I–IV of NREM sleep) and inhibition (during REM sleep). In dreams, we imagine that we move but we do not. The sequence of these stages is schematically represented in the polygraph channel and sample tracings are also shown. Three variables are used to distinguish these states: the electromyograph (EMG), which is the highest in waking, intermediate in NREM sleep, and lowest in REM sleep; the electroencephalogram (EEG) and electrooculogram (EOG), which are both activated in waking and REM sleep, and inactivated in NREM sleep. Each sample record is about 20 sec long. Other subjective and objective state variables are described in the three lower channels

70

The sensori-motor aspects of sleep may be seen in other conditions such us narcosis and hypothermia but are distinguished from these non-sleep states by their relative reversibility: the increased response threshold to stimuli can always be overcome, and sleeping animals can quickly regain both upright postures and alertness following sufficiently strong stimuli. The distinction of sleep from states of torpor (in those cold-blooded animals that cannot regulate their core body temperature) has a similar evolutionary history to the neural structures mediating the electrographic signs of sleep. Critical brain parts include the cerebral cortex and thalamus whose complex evolution underlies the distinctive EEG features of sleep in the higher vertebrate mammals. Sleep constitutes the state of entry to and exit from hibernation in those mammalian species who regulate temperature at lower levels during winter.

In humans, it is now clear that mental activity undergoes a progressive and systematic reorganization throughout sleep. On first falling asleep individuals may progressively lose awareness of the outside world and experience micro-hallucinations and illusions of movement of the body in space; after sleep onset, mental activity persists but is described as thought-like and perseverative if it can be recalled at all upon awakening. These four correlated features − (1) the assumption of recumbent, or inert postures; (2) the increase in response threshold to stimulation; (3) the evolution of distinctive electroen-cephalographic features; and (4) the decrease in efficiency of mental activity − together constitute the fundamental features of the initial stages of sleep in humans. All animals whose sleep may be properly distinguished from states of torpor share the first three features.

Physiological aspects of sleep

The conditions described above do not persist throughout the sleep of most animals; rather, there is a complex reorganization of behavioural, physio-logical, and psychological events within each sleep bout. To detect this process, it is convenient to record the brain activity by means of an electroen-cephalogram (EEG) from the surface of the head (or directly from the cortical structures of the brain), to record the movement of the eyes by means of the electrooculogram (EOG), and to record muscle tone by means of the electromyogram (EMG). These three electrographic parameters allow one to distinguish sleep from waking and to distinguish two distinctive and cyclically recurrent phases within sleep, NREM (non-rapid eye movement) and REM (rapid eye movement) sleep. NREM, or synchronized sleep, is characterized by a change in the EEG from a low-amplitude, high-frequency pattern to a high-amplitude, low-frequency pattern. The degree to which the EEG is progressively synchronized (that is, of high voltage and low frequency) can be subdivided into four stages in humans (see Table 1). At the same time that

Table 1 EEG frequency and voltage characteristics of NREM sleep stages I–IV

Sleep stage	Frequency	Voltage
I	4–7 cycles per second (cps) (theta range)	arrhythmic $< 50\,\text{mV}$
II	12–15 cps (spindle complexes)	peaks at 100 mV
III	1–4 cps (with spindle complexes)	$> 100\,\text{mV}$
IV	1–3 cps (delta range)	150–250 mV

the EEG frequency is decreasing and the voltage increasing, muscle tone progressively declines and may be lost in most of the somatic musculature.

After varying amounts of time (depending upon the size of the animal and its brain), this progressive set of changes in the EEG reverses itself and the EEG finally resumes the low voltage, fast character previously seen in waking. Instead of waking, however, behavioural sleep persists; muscle tone (at first passively decreased) is now actively inhibited; and there arise in the electrooculogram stereotyped bursts of saccadic eye movement called rapid eye movements (the REMs, which give this sleep state the name REM sleep). This phase of sleep has also been called activated sleep (to signal the EEG low voltage, high frequency shared by REM and waking) and paradoxical sleep (to signal the maintenance of increased threshold to arousal in the face of the activated brain).

In all mammals (including aquatic, arboreal, and flying species) sleep is organized in this cyclic fashion: sleep is initiated by NREM and punctuated by REM at regular intervals. Most animals compose a sleep bout out of three or more such cycles, and in mature humans the average nocturnal sleep period consists of four to five such cycles, each of 90–100 min duration. After a prolonged period of wake activity (as in humans), the first cycles are characterized by NREM phase enhancement (a preponderance of high-voltage, slow wave activity) while the last cycles show more REM phase enhancement (low-voltage, fast wave activity). The period is of fixed length across any and all sleep periods.

Recent progress in the cellular neurophysiology of sleep

Since the early 1960s the neurobiological mechanisms of sleep have been investigated in experimental animals using lesion, stimulation, and single-cell recording techniques. The results are of great psychological significance because they demonstrate a clear correspondence between the states of the

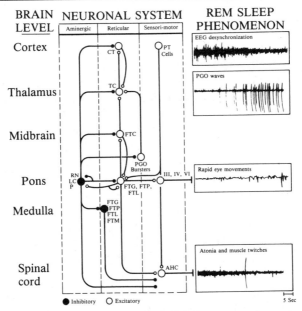

Figure 2 Schematic representation of the REM sleep generation process. The electrographic signs of REM sleep in the cat are shown in the four boxes on the right. A distributed network involves cells at many brain levels (left). The network is represented as comprising three neuronal systems (centre) that mediate REM sleep electrographic phenomena (right). Postulated inhibitory connections are shown as *solid circles*; postulated excitatory connections as *open circles*. In this diagram no distinction is made between neurotransmission and neuromodulatory functions of the depicted neurons. It should be noted that the actual synaptic signs of many of the aminergic and reticular pathways remain to be demonstrated, and in many cases, the neuronal architecture is known to be far more complex than indicated here (e.g., the thalamas and cortex). Two additive effects of the marked reduction in firing rate by aminergic neurons at REM sleep onset are postulated: disinhibition (through removal of negative restraint) and facilitation (through positive feedback). The net result is strong tonic and phasic activation of reticular and sensori-motor neurons in REM sleep. REM sleep phenomena are postulated to be mediated as follows: EEG desynchronization results from a net tonic increase in reticular, thalamocortical, and cortical neuronal firing rates. PGO waves (see text) are the result of tonic disinhibition and phasic excitation of burst cells in the lateral pontomesencephalic tegmentum. Rapid eye movements are the consequence of physic firing by reticular and vestibular cells; the latter (not shown) directly excite oculomotor neurons. Muscular atonia is the consequence of tonic postsynaptic inhibition of spinal anterior horn cells by the pontomedullary reticular formation. Muscle twitches occur when excitation by reticular and pyramidal tract motoneurons phasically overcomes the tonic inhibition of the anterior horn cells. Anatomical abbreviations: RN, raphé nuclei; LC, locus coeruleus; P, peribrachial region; FTC, central tegmental field; FTG, gigantocellular tegmental field; FTL, lateral tegmental field; FTM, magnocellular tegmental field; FTP, parvocellular tegmental field; TC, thalamocortical; CT, cortical; PT cell, pyramidal cell; III, oculomotor; IV, trochlear; V, trigmenial motor nuclei; AHC, anterior horn cell

Source: Modified from Hobson, Lydic, and Baghdoyan, 1986

73

brain and the states of the mind. While debate continues on the precise architecture and dynamics of the NREM–REM sleep cycle control system, there is widespread agreement on the following points: the critical neurons are localized in the brain stem, principally the pontine tegmentum (as Jouvet originally suggested in 1962), but the critical neurons are more widely distributed and more heterogeneous than originally thought. They are gathered in numerous nuclei and have a diverse chemical constitution and connectivity (see Figure 2). This explains one of the great puzzles of sleep research: why REM sleep, whose control is clearly localized in the pons, can be neither completely abolished by local electrolytic lesions nor consistently evoked by local electrical stimulation. Aminergic neurones enhance waking and suppress REM sleep. Thus drugs which augment noradrenergic and/or serotonergic activity tend to increase arousal but impede REM sleep, suggesting a cholinergic-aminergic, push-pull oscillatory system of sleeping and waking (Karczmar, Longo, & De Carolis, 1970). Recent experiments indicate that REM sleep can be increased for over a week following a single microscopic injection of cholinergic drug into the brain stem. Cholinergic neurons enhance some REM sleep events, and all or part of the REM sleep phase can be cholinergically stimulated.

DREAMING

Dreaming is a distinctive mental state that occurs periodically in normal human sleep. Typical dream reports include such psychological features as hallucinations, delusions, cognitive abnormalities, emotional intensification, and amnesia. These five remarkable features of dreaming have invited its comparison to abnormal states of mind occurring during waking in certain clinical conditions, especially schizophrenia and the organic mental syndromes, in particular delirium (see Table 2). The exploration of dreaming therefore constitutes not only an aspect of mind–body (psychophysiological)

Table 2 Some formal cognitive aspects of dreaming

Mental faculty	Dream characteristics
Orientation	Discontinuity and incongruity of times, places and persons
Memory	Amnesia for over 95% of dreams
Thinking	Insight and logic impaired
	Inferences uncertain and inaccurate
Sensory perceptions	Intense visual illusion
	Continuous illusion of motion
Visceral perceptions	Weak or absent sense of smell, taste and pain
Emotions	Labile with intensification of anxiety, anger and elation
	Weak or absent sadness, shame and guilt

interaction but also a model approach to the study of mental illness. An obvious problem is that the unconformable nature of all subjective experience is compounded by difficult access to the mind in sleep. The recent development of sleep laboratory techniques has given the study of dreaming a more instrumental and systematic character, and the emerging picture encourages psychophysiological integration.

Psychological features of dreaming

Dreams are characterized by vivid and fully formed hallucinatory imagery with the visual sensory domain predominant: auditory, tactile, and movement sensations are also prominent in most dream reports. Compared with the intense involvement of these sensori-motor domains, taste and smell are underrepresented and reports of pain are exceedingly rare despite the involvement of dreamers in frightening and even physically mutilating scenarios.

Dreaming is properly considered delusional because subjects have virtually no insight regarding the true nature of the state in which they have these unusual sensory experiences. The tendency is thus great to consider dream events as if they were completely real even though they are promptly recognized as fabrications when recalled in subsequent waking states. This is all the more surprising since the uncritical belief in the reality of dream events must overcome high degrees of improbability and even physical impossibility.

The lack of insight that makes dreams delusional is part of a broader set of cognitive disturbances. Dreams are characterized by marked uncertainties (with explicit vagueness); discontinuities (with unexplained changes of subject, actions, and setting); impossibilities (with defiance of physical law) and improbabilities; and incongruities (with social inappropriateness and cognitive illogicality). Dream characters and dream objects may be banal or altogether fantastic and impossible collages of existing reality; they may behave normally or indulge in the most absurd, improbable, or impossible actions in settings either familiar or bearing only the faintest resemblances to those of real life. To explain these unique and remarkable dream features illogical thought processes such as non sequiturs, post-hoc explanations, and mythical, metaphorical, and symbolic interpretations are the norm.

Memory undergoes a paradoxical intensification and suppression: recall is intensified within the dream as remote characters, scenes, events, and concerns are knitted into the fanciful and evanescent fabric of the dream. Dreams can thus be said to be hypermnesic (extraordinary memory recall) within the state itself; this increased access to memory within the state of dreaming contrasts markedly with the virtual impossibility of recovering the dream product after the state has terminated. On awakening even from a dream in progress, subjects have difficulty holding the vivid experiences in short-term memory long enough to give a report or transcribe the dream

75

scenario in detail. It can be conservatively stated that at least 95 per cent of all dream mentation is totally forgotten.

Emotion fluctuates widely in association with the abnormal and vivid mental content of dreaming: anxiety, fear, and surprise are common affects which undergo marked intensification during dreams. Obsessional concerns are common with dreamers focusing their worry about nudity, missed trains, unpacked suitcases, and a host of other incomplete arrangements. Depressive affects are markedly underrepresented, with shame and guilt playing a relatively small part.

The definition and characterization of dreaming given here serves to differentiate it from other kinds of mental activities that may occur in sleep. Fleeting images accompanied by the sensation of falling (but unsustained by a narrative plot and sequential action) characterize mental activity at sleep onset. Once sleep is established, mentation assumes a thought-like character which is usually perseverative and unprogressive as the sleeper reviews daytime activities and concerns in a persistent, repetitious manner. Such sleep "thinking" is unaccompanied by either vivid visual imagery or bizarre cognitive feature. Sustained dream scenarios occur only after these two forms of mental activity have subsided. Dreaming then alternates with thought-like mentation at 90–100-minute intervals throughout the night. Recall of dreams and other forms of mental activity in sleep depends upon prompt awakening from the state in which the mental activity occurs; retention of such recall further depends upon the instrumental act of verbally reporting or transcribing the dream narration.

Dreaming and REM sleep

In 1953 Aserinsky and Kleitman noted that the sleep of children was interrupted periodically by activation of the EEG and by bursts of saccadic eye movement, the so-called rapid eye movements, or REMs, of sleep (see Figures 1 and 2). Dement (1955) confirmed the hypothesis that these periods of brain activation during sleep were correlated with dreaming as defined above. When normal subjects were aroused from REM sleep, they gave detailed reports of dream activity. The capacity to recall dreams appeared to be related to the nature of the awakening process; subjects who learned to obtain a fully aroused state without moving increased their recall capacity. Within the REM period, dream intensity tended to parallel the intensity of other physiological events, especially the eye movements; arousal during REM sleep with the eye movement activity yielded reports fulfilling the definition of dreaming given here in 90–95 per cent of the cases. When scored for vividness, emotionality, and imagined physical activity, measures were correlated positively with the quantitative intensity of the eye movement in the REM sleep just prior to awakening. Awakening during REM sleep without eye movement yielded reports of lesser intensity in about 70 per cent of the awakenings. These figures dropped to 5–10 per cent when awakenings were made during non-REM sleep.

Awakenings from non-REM sleep yielded reports of mental activity in about 50 per cent of the trials, but a large proportion of these reports were of perseverative, thought-like mental activity. Reports qualitatively indistinguishable from dreaming were obtained from stage I sleep at sleep onset, a phase of sleep without sustained eye movements; but these reports were quantitatively less impressive in duration and intensity than those obtained from emergent REM sleep periods later in the night.

Estimations of dream duration correlate positively with the time spent in REM sleep prior to arousal. When subjects were aroused after only 5 minutes of REM sleep, they gave shorter reports; after 15 minutes had elapsed, reports were considerably longer and more detailed. Thus it would appear, despite intensification and contraction of duration estimates within individual dream scenarios, that overall correlation between time estimation of dream duration and real time elapsed in REM sleep is quite good.

To test the resistance of memory to dreams, awakenings were performed in the non-REM sleep phase at intervals following the termination of REM. The incidence of reported dreams dropped to non-REM levels within 5 minutes of the end of a REM cycle, indicating the extremely fragile state of memory and highlighting the strong state dependency of recall upon arousal from REM sleep.

Psychophysiological theories of dreaming

The simplest and most direct approach to the correlation of dream mentation with the physiological state of the sleeping brain is to assume a formal isomorphism between the subjective and objective levels of description. By isomorphism is meant a similarity of form in the psychological and physiological domains. For example, subjective experience of visually formed imagery in dreams implicates the activation of the same perceptual elements in the visual system that operate in the waking state. Other details of psychophysiological correlation are assumed to obey the same general law; for example, the vivid hallucinated sensation of moving within dreams is assumed to be related to patterned activation of motor systems and those central brain structures that control the perception of position and changes in position of the body in space during the waking state. When we look at the physiological level for patterned activation of the visual motor and vestibular systems, we find that powerful, highly coordinated excitatory processes are recordable in oculomotor nerves, the middle ear, and visual sensory centres.

To be fully adequate, a psychophysiological hypothesis has to account for the following processes (see Figure 3a,b).

1 *Activation* The brain has to be turned on and kept internally activated

to support dream mentation throughout the REM sleep episode. A possible mechanism is the disinhibition of sensori-motor circuits (see Figure 2 and Figure 3b).

2 *Input blockade* Input from the outside world to an internally activated brain has to be prevented in order for sleep and the illusions of dreaming to be maintained. This is accomplished in at least two ways. One is the inhibition of the group Ia nerves, which impedes access to the central nervous system from signals of peripheral origin; this presynaptic inhibition has also been recorded throughout the brain stem and thalamus. The second mechanism for excluding sensory input is obstruction which occupies the higher levels of sensory circuits with internally generated messages.

3 *Output blockade* The internally activated and actively deafferented brain must also quell motor outputs to prevent the disruption of sleep by stimulation created by movement and to halt the enactment of dreamed motor commands. This is accomplished by postsynaptic inhibition of motoneurons in the spinal cord and brain stem. By these three processes, the brain is thus made ready to process information arising from within, to exclude data coming from without, and not to act upon the internally generated information.

4 *Internal signal generation* It remains to provide the activated but disconnected brain with internal signals which it then processes as if they came from the outside world. This appears to occur in part by a mechanism intrinsic to brain activation: the reciprocal interaction of aminergic and cholinergic neurons in the brain stem. In most mammals including humans, the so-called PGO waves – P, pons, G, (lateral) geniculate; and O, occipital cortex – present themselves as candidates for an internally generated information signal arising at the level of the pontine brain stem (see Figure 2, second box on right, PGO waves). In association with oculomotor activity, strong pulses of excitation are conducted to visual and association cortices and the thalamus. It is now known that these PGO waves are generated by cellular activity which faithfully replicates generated eye movements at the level of the brain stem. Thus not only is internal information generated but also the information has the accompanying eye movements to create spatial specificity. According to the activation-synthesis hypothesis of dreaming, the now autoactivated and autostimulated brain processes these signals and interprets them in terms of information stored in memory.

The precise neural basis of the cognitive disturbances occurring in dreaming is not understood. It is tempting to see these failures as perhaps related to the cessation of activity in the aminergic neurons (which enhance waking and suppress REM sleep). This arrest of aminergic neuronal activity would affect the entire brain by depriving it of the tonic modulatory influence of norepinephrine (noradrenaline) and serotonin. It is speculated that this tonic modulatory influence may be essential to attentional processes, including the capacity to organize information in a logical and coherent manner and to achieve full self-awareness. In the absence of external cues and internal modulatory influences, the activated forebrain would interpret its internally generated signals as if they were real. By a similar mechanism it may be speculated that the synthesized dream product is unremembered. That is, the activated forebrain circuits which mediated the dream experience are simply not instructed to keep a record of the transaction. Aminergic interneurons are also postulated to regulate mnemonic instruction as they send signals to create memory to the vast postsynaptic domain in waking (when they are active) but not in dreaming (where they are inactive). Current models of learning and memory at the cellular level evoke the intervention of an aminergic interneuron. Thus, the attribution of dream amnesia to the loss of aminergic modulation is consistent with these hypotheses.

This activation-synthesis model of dreaming and the reciprocal interaction theory of sleep cycle control to which it is linked are both incomplete and controversial. They both represent working hypotheses about the

REM SLEEP AND DREAMING

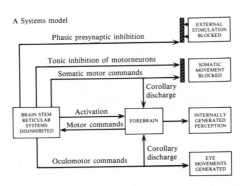

Figure 3a Systems model As a result of disinhibition caused by cessation of aminergic neuronal firing, brain stem reticular systems become autoactive. Their outputs have effects including depolarization of afferent terminals causing phasic presynaptic inhibition and blockade of external stimuli, especially during the burst of REM; postsynaptic hyperpolarization causing tonic inhibition of moto-neurons which effectively counteract concomitant motor commands so that somatic movement is blocked. Only the oculomotor commands are read out as eye movements because the moto-neurons are not inhibited. The forebrain, activated by the reticular formation and also aminergically disinhibited, receives efferent copy or corollary discharge information about somatic motor and oculomotor commands from which it may synthesize such internally generated perceptions as visual imagery and the sensation of movement, both which typify dream mentation. The forebrain may, in turn, generate its own motor commands which help to perpetuate the process via positive feedback to the reticular formation

fundamental physiology of sleep and the way in which that physiology may help us to understand unique features of the dream process. The attribution of automaticity to the control system and the feature of randomness in the information generator model should not be taken to exclude the meaningful nature of the synthetic process carried out by the dreaming brain. By definition, the brain/mind of each dreamer is obliged to make as much sense as is possible of its internally generated signals under the adverse working conditions of REM sleep. Thus, the dream product for each individual may contain unique stylistic psychological features and concerns and may thus be worthy of scrutiny by the individual to review life strategies. But the new theory challenges the psychoanalytic idea that the many meaningless aspects of dream mentation are the result of an active effort to disguise the meaning of unconscious wishes (which are in turn postulated to be the driving force of dreaming). Instead, it ascribes these defective cognitive properties of dreaming to unusual operating features of the internally activated, autostimulated brain during REM sleep.

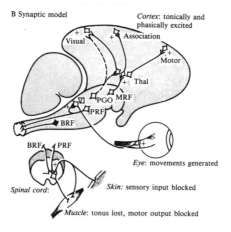

Figure 3b Synaptic model Some of the directly and indirectly disinhibited neuronal systems are schematized together with their supposed contributions to REM sleep phenomena. At the level of the brain stem, five neuronal types are illustrated: midbrain reticular neurons (MRF) projecting to thalamus convey tonic and phasic activating signals rostrally; burst cells in the peribrachial region (PGO) convey phasic activation and specific eye movement information to the geniculate body and cortex (dashed line indicates uncertainty of direct projection); pontine reticular formation (PRF) neurons transmit phasic activation signals to oculomotor neurons (VI) and spinal cord which generate eye movements, twitches of extremities, and presynaptic inhibition; bulbar reticular formation (BRF) neurons send tonic hyperpolarizing signals to motor neurons in spinal cord. As a consequence of these descending influences, sensory input and motor output are blocked at the level of the spinal cord. At the level of the forebrain, visual association and motor cortex neurons all receive tonic and phasic activation signals from non-specific and specific thalamic relay cells

FUNCTIONS OF SLEEP AND DREAMING

The main achievements since the mid-1960s have been in describing previously unsuspected sleep phenomena and in detailing the neural mechanisms by which sleep is controlled. While incomplete and still controversial, schemata of the type outlined earlier in the chapter will almost certainly be more confidently established in the near future. Completely without definitive supporting evidence, however, are the multiple functional theories that the diversity of new findings relevant to sleep phenomena and sleep mechanisms have produced.

These theories can be conveniently considered in four categories: the behavioural, the developmental, the metabolic, and the informational. (The informational level is discussed later in the chapter).

At the *behavioural level*, it is clear that sleep serves to suppress activity at times of the day when the likelihood of accomplishing a given specific goal is relatively low; finding food (self-preservation) and mates (furthering of the species) are clearly less likely to go well in sighted animals when light levels are low. Such activity also has a high energy cost in homeothermic animals when temperature is low. Thus the efficiency of sleep is clear (at the behavioural level). Correspondingly, the enforced nature of sleep and its relation to nesting activity clearly serves to unite animals in a family or pair-bonded situation that may foster sexual behaviour and promote nurturance and development of the young. Incredibly, scientists who study animal behaviour (ethologists) have not conducted systematic investigations of such ecological notions of sleep. The recognition of sleep as a behaviour by ethologists, especially neuroethologists, has not yet occurred. The current development of remote and portable monitoring systems makes this a promising area of investigation.

At the *developmental level*, it is certainly significant that sleep is the major state of existence in the life of the immature animal. For example, the newborn human sleeps 16 hours a day and half of this period is devoted to REM. This indicates not only a preponderance of sleep in the immature animal but also a disproportionate allowance of time to the REM phase. The newborn human devotes a full 8 hours to REM sleep each day. In further contradistinction to the adult profile, REM sleep may occur immediately at sleep onset. As indicated earlier, the length of the cycle is a function of brain size within and across species so that, in the newborn human infant, cycle length is 45 minutes as against 90 minutes in the adult state.

The high proportion of sleep in REM at birth is complemented by even higher levels during the last trimester of mammalian life in utero. During later stages of development the total amount of sleep will decrease to one-half and the amount of each sleep devoted to REM will decrease to one-quarter of the neonatal level. At the same time the period length of the NREM–REM cycle doubles (from 45 to 90 minutes). In immature animals both NREM and

REM sleep show important quantitative differences from the adult state: slow waves are less well developed at birth and become more distinctively differentiated as brain and behavioural competence increase. The muscle inhibition of REM sleep is considerably less well established at birth than at maturity and the phasic muscle twitches, which are only faintly visible in most adult mammals, are dramatically and clearly evident in the immature members of the species. Thus both the allocation of time and the qualitative appearance of sleep change dramatically during development.

A function of REM sleep for the developing organisms could be guaranteed activation of neural circuits underlying elemental behaviours. It is attractive to think of the evolutionary advantages of guaranteeing the organized activation of the complex systems of the brain before the organism has developed the full capability of testing them in the real world. An associated idea is that of behavioural rehearsal. In the developing and in the adult animal REM sleep could guarantee maintenance of circuits critical for survival whether or not they were called upon for use during the wake state.

At the *metabolic level*, the fact that the early cycles are predominantly composed of slow wave sleep has given rise to the notion that this sleep stage may serve to rest the body and be responsive to the duration of the preceding wake period. The low-voltage fast (or REM) phase of sleep (which is recovered later) may have more to do with anabolic processes and be related to the function of the brain itself.

The recurrent cycles of NREM and REM sleep are accompanied by major changes in all physiological systems of the body. During NREM sleep there are decreases in blood pressure, heart rate, and respiratory rate and pulsatile release of growth and sex hormones from the pituitary. The concomitance of these events gives further credence to the notion that NREM sleep may be functionally associated with constructive processes benefiting the somatic tissues.

REM sleep is associated with activation of other physiological functions: heart rate, blood pressure, and respiratory rate and irregularity all increase. Penile erection in males and clitoral engorgement in females accompany the brain and autonomic activation of this phase, and although the somatic musculature is actively inhibited, small twitches of the facial, digital, and even major proximal skeletal muscles may be observed. It is unlikely that these features simply denote a functional state of rest.

It has been demonstrated that slow wave sleep is associated with appreciable savings of energy in many neural structures. The decrease in action potential generation by many central neurons is associated with decreases in cerebral blood flow and cerebral metabolism. It seems unlikely, however, that such modest energy savings can be the sole or major function of sleep since they are all lost or reversed during the REM phase. In REM, however, the arrest of firing by aminergic neurons could allow replenishment of neurotransmitter levels or of synthetic enzymes needed to assure the synaptic efficiency of attentional systems in the wake state.

SPECIFIC FUNCTIONAL HYPOTHESES

Effects of sleep deprivation

Because mental lapses and fatigue are the well-known sequelae of even moderate sleep deprivation, common sense has long held that sleep is as essential to effective information processing as it is to energy homeostasis. But, because convincing experimental models of these phenomena have not been available, the underlying pathophysiology (functional changes) of the deficit states and the mediating variables of sleep's supposed benefits have not been elucidated. The discovery of sleep's periodic NREM and REM phases retarded progress in this area, by inducing scientists to make fruitless attempts to differentiate between a hypothetical energy-restoration function for NREM sleep and a cognitive or information-processing function for REM sleep.

Long-term sleep deprivation in rats has recently been shown to produce impaired thermoregulation, metabolic dyscontrol, and death. Studies by Rechtschaffen and co-workers (1989a, 1989b) demonstrated this by selectively depriving rats of either REM sleep or both NREM and REM sleep (Gilliland, Bergmann, & Rechtschaffen, 1989; Kushida, Bergmann, & Rechtschaffen, 1989). After one week of total sleep deprivation, rats show a progressive weight loss, which occurs even in the face of increased food intake. The progressive weight loss, which becomes more pronounced after two weeks, appears to be a syndrome of metabolic dyscontrol, which causes more and more calories to be consumed in a vain attempt to restore lost energy homeostasis. When deprivation is stopped, recovery is prompt and complete (Everson et al., 1989). En route to each rat's demise at about four weeks of deprivation, body weight plummets, while food consumption soars, and the body temperature becomes progressively more unstable.

These observations provide an excellent model for the investigation of what appears to be a progressive failure of energy-regulating mechanisms within the brain. One attractive hypothesis is that sleep deprivation causes a progressive loss of aminergic synaptic firing power, resulting from overdriving the sympathetic system on the one hand, and denying the respite from neurotransmitter release that normally occurs in sleep. According to this interpretation, aminergic discharge and/or transmitter release would increase as an initial response to sleep deprivation. However, as the sleep-deprived brain becomes more and more depleted of its sympathetic neurotransmitters, first cognitive, then thermal, and finally homeostatic caloric systems would fail. These and other hypotheses involving sleep-dependent neuroendocrine responses (such as growth hormone release) can be tested in the new sleep paradigm.

Temperature regulation

Sleep onset normally occurs on the descending limb of the curve describing the circadian body temperature rhythm, and a further drop in body temperature occurs with the first episode of NREM sleep. Furthermore, two distinct thermal adaptations, shallow torpor (a temperature drop occurring daily in small mammals) and hibernation (a more profound and prolonged seasonal drop in body temperature) occur during NREM sleep (Heller, Glotzbach, Grahn, & Radehe, 1988). These facts combine to favour the view that sleep is part of a continuum of diverse energy conservation strategies used by mammals to cope with varying levels and sources of heat and light. Whatever benefits sleep may accrue for tomorrow, one clear function is to conserve calories for today.

In addition to a drop in body temperature, reduced responsiveness to changes in ambient temperature is also observed in NREM sleep; shivering in response to cold and sweating in response to heat are both diminished. Heller and co-workers at Stanford (1988) and Parmeggiani and colleagues in Bologna (1988) have shown that the responsiveness of temperature sensor neurons in the preoptic hypothalamus dips to a lower level in NREM sleep than in waking, and bottoms out in REM sleep. In sleep, the animal apparently changes its behaviour as a substitute for its neuronal thermostat – an unlikely high-cost manoeuvre for a small short-term calorie saving.

Daily observations in human body temperature of $1.5°C$ were observed in the first phase of sleep research and led to the discovery of the circadian rhythm (Aschoff, 1965b). The circadian rhythm of temperature has been shown to be tightly coupled to the circadian rhythm of sleep and waking, and the degree to which these can be dissociated continues to be debated. The dual oscillator theory suggests there is one oscillator for body temperature and another for sleep. While the two oscillators can be dissociated both surgically and chemically (Jouvet et al., 1988), the cellular and molecular basis of the circadian oscillator and the mechanism of its coupling to the other oscillators remains to be fathomed.

Immune system

It is well known that humans with an infectious disease become sleepy, but the mechanism of this effect and its functional significance are not understood. Is this a consequence of increasing demands upon the sympathetic nervous system and upon energy metabolism, with more calories diverted to defensive processes? The work in this newly developing area of sleep and immune function interaction are studying particularly the capacity of interleukin-1 to promote sleep.

These experiments grew out of major work initiated by John Pappenheimer and colleagues (1975), which identified the NREM sleep-promoting factor (S) in the spinal fluid of sleep-deprived goats and rabbits as a muramyl dipeptide (MDP). Muramyl peptides are not found in brain cells but are the building blocks of bacterial cell walls. They are responsible for raising body temperature (pyrogenic) and stimulating the immune system, in addition to having sleep-inducing effects (somnogenic), which appear to be at least partially independent of their pyrogenicity (Krueger, Walter, & Levin, 1985b). One particularly intriguing finding is the capacity of MDP to compete with serotonin at its binding sites on both the central nervous system and immune system cells, suggesting a common mechanism linking MDP's sleep-promoting and immunostimulatory effects (Silverman & Karnovsky, 1989).

Interleukin-1 is an immunostimulatory and somnogenic peptide which is endogenous, being produced by brain glial cells and macrophages. Both interleukin-1 and MDP enhance tumorcidal and bacteriocidal activity. Interleukin-1 alters sleep in a manner similar to muramyl peptides; time spent in NREM sleep, amplitude of the EEG slow waves, and duration of individual episodes of sleep are all increased by this compound (Krueger, Walter, Dinarello, & Chedid, 1985a). However, because time spent in REM sleep is markedly decreased by both compounds, their contribution to the physiology of normal sleep remains uncertain.

Cognition

Work on the cognitive neuroscience of sleep is tantalizing, but most of its promise remains unfulfilled. Early results indicated that learning (i.e., conditioned avoidance) in rats is followed by increases in REM sleep and is impaired by deprivation of REM sleep (Bloch, 1973; Fishbein, Kastaniotis, & Chattman, 1974; Smith, Kitahama, Valatx, & Jouvet, 1974). Efforts to further detail these findings revealed that the increase in REM sleep following conditioned avoidance is quite prolonged (Smith, Young, & Young, 1980; Smith & Lapp, 1986), and that REM sleep must occur at particular times after training in order for learning to occur.

In studies with humans, two interesting new findings using the deprivation technique substantiate the idea that sleep improves cognitive competence. Mikulincer, Babkoff, Caspy, & Sing (1989) showed that measures of attention, concentration, affect, and motivation declined with increasing sleep loss and that all these measures were powerfully sensitive to time of day. The problem with such studies is that their strongly correlative findings (brains do not work well when sleepy) do not establish the causal hypothesis (brains work well because of sleep).

Contrary to common sense and most sleep research findings, the provocative theory of Crick and Mitchison (1983) states that we have REM sleep (and dreams) to forget. The theory addresses a long-standing problem in neuropsychology: how brains distinguish between trivial and important associations and memories. (Hartley, 1801; Luria, 1968). There are two different ways through interactions in the brain that such sorting could occur. Procedural memories (dealing with a series of actions) might be reinforced through the interaction of a fixed repertoire of motor commands (issued automatically by the brain stem during REM sleep) and synaptic hotspot residues of the day's sensori-motor experience. Declarative memories might be reinforced through interaction with fixed action programmes of emotional and vegetative behaviours programmed in the limbic systems. Our dreams clearly reflect some such integrative process: they are constantly animated and we move through diverse settings, combining both recent and remote experience in an emotional climate often fraught with strong feelings of anxiety and fear.

The problem with these attractive ideas is that they are most difficult to test experimentally in living animals. Thus one of the most attractive aspects of the Crick-Mitchison theory is its heuristic resort to neural net behaviour in computerized brain simulations. Another option for the cognitive neuroscience of sleep is a more imaginative use of "experiments of nature", for

	Waking	NREM sleep	REM sleep
Aminergic	LC, DRN		
Cholinergic	Ch 1–4 Ch 5		

Figure 4a State-dependent changes in aminergic and cholinergic neuronal function. Schematic representation of progressive decrease of aminergic neurotransmitter release in cerebral cortex as animal passes from waking through NREM to REM sleep. Cortical concentrations of norepinphrine (noradrenaline) and serotonin are highest in waking, lowest in REM sleep, and intermediate in NREM sleep. Top panel illustrates sagittal sections of the brain with aminergic neurons of nucleus locus coeruleus (noradrenerigic) and dorsal raphe nucleus (serotonergic). Bottom panel illustrates cholinergic neurons in basal forebrain and peribrachial pontine tegmentum. Cholinergic neurons release levels of acetycholine as high in REM as they are in waking; release in NREM sleep is lower

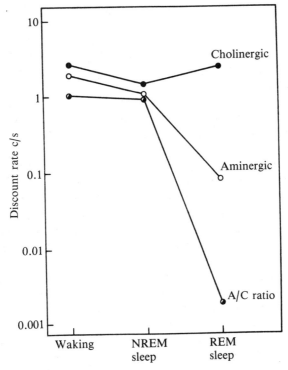

Figure 4b State-dependent changes in aminergic-to-cholinergic ratio. Quantitative estimate of aminergic (A) and cholinergic (C) neurotransmitter concentrations may be derived from single-unit recording studies and by direct and indirect measurements of neurotransmitter release. Because values are similar and parallel in waking and NREM sleep but diverge in REM sleep, the ratio of the two values amplifies the difference between REM and the other two states. Values of A are computed by averaging mean rate of putatively noradrenergic and serotonergic neurons recorded by microelectrodes in brain stem of cats. Inferred decrease in release has been confirmed voltametrically, for serotonin, in waking and in REM sleep. Values of C are computed by averaging mean rate of unidentified cortical neurons. These estimates are compatible with direct measurements of acetylcholine release from cerebral cortex

example, the clinical study of patients with brain lesions. While brain-stem-lesion patients lose REM sleep entirely, cortical lesion patients lose only dreaming. Are there differences in what such different kinds of patients can learn (or at least not forget)?

When the metabolic and developmental implications of our rapidly increasing knowledge of sleep mechanism are considered at the *informational level*, other intriguing theories can be enunciated. For example, if the brain is only slightly decreased in level of activity during slow-wave sleep and increases activity again (during REM sleep), but with a change of information processing mode during REM sleep, it is possible to imagine that later stages of the learning process may be enhanced during sleep. To be more specific, the cerebral cortex may benefit differentially from the NREM and REM phases of sleep. The activity of aminergic brain stem neurons (and direct measurements of neurotransmitter release in the forebrain) indicated that the activated states of waking and REM sleep are at diametrically opposite poles: the ratio of aminergic activity (high in waking and lowest in REM sleep) to cholinergic activity (high in both waking and in REM sleep) therefore places NREM sleep in a functionally intermediary position (see Figure 4a,b).

Since aminergic and cholinergic neurotransmitters not only influence neural events at the membrane level but also influence the metabolic activity of the cytoplasm and nucleus (via second messengers), it is the postsynaptic change in mode of operation of the entire brain that may contain the secret of the functional specificity of NREM and REM sleep. Sleep could be thus a programme for the comparison of genetically determined organizational priorities of the brain with the external experience of the animal. The upshot of this idea is that information already stored in memory is compared with recent inputs such that the memory stores can be corrected and updated. Related notions include consolidation of memory and the elimination of unwanted or spurious information.

Now that the metabolic differentiation of REM sleep and waking has been detailed at the level of single cells and specific neurotransmitters, it is possible to envisage a new line of functional investigations in which the consequences of metabolic switching can be specifically tested with respect to protein metabolism in the brain.

CONCLUSION

Modern sleep research has evolved from an early, descriptive phase in the human sleep lab through an increasingly detailed and precise analysis of the cellular and molecular mechanisms that regulate the NREM–REM cycle in experimental animals. The fruit of this two-pronged attack is a completely new approach to our understanding of exceptional mental states, like dreaming with its many formal similarities to mental illness, in terms of specific brain processes. Now attention is being focused upon functional questions in studies of animals subjected to experimental deprivation and in experiments of nature which result in human sleep disorders. Evidence from all these sources converges to suggest that sleep is a complex, neurological strategy for simultaneously promoting energy regulation and automatic information processing by the brain.

ACKNOWLEDGEMENTS

This chapter is based on articles by the author, which first appeared in the following publications.

Hobson, J. A. (1987). Dreaming. In G. Adelman (Ed.) *Encyclopedia of neuroscience* (vol. 1, pp. 338–340). Boston, MA: Birkhauser.

Hobson, J. A. (1987). Sleep. In G. Adelman (Ed.) *Encyclopedia of neuroscience* (vol. 2, pp. 1097–1101). Boston, MA: Birkhauser.

Hobson, J. A. (1988). Homeostasis and heteroplasticity: Functional significance of behavioral state sequences. In R. Lydic & J. F. Biebuyck (Eds) *The clinical physiology of sleep* (pp. 199–200). Bethesda, MD: American Physiological Society.

Hobson, J. A. (1990). Sleep and dreaming. *Journal of Neuroscience, 10,* 371–382.

FURTHER READING

Bootzin, R., Kihistrom, J., & Schachter, D. (Eds) (1990). *Sleep and cognition.* Washington, DC: American Psychological Association.

Cohen, D. B. (1979). *Sleep and dreaming: Origins, nature and functions.* Oxford: Pergamon.

Hobson, J. A. (1988). *The dreaming brain.* New York: Basic Books.

Hobson, J. A. (1989). *Sleep.* New York: Scientific American Library.

REFERENCES

Aschoff, J. (1965a). *Circadian clocks.* Amsterdam: North-Holland.

Aschoff, J. (1965b). Circadian rhythms in man. *Science, 148,* 1427–1432.

Aserinsky, E., & Kleitman, N. (1953). Regularly occurring periods of eye motility and concomitant phenomena during sleep. *Science, 118,* 273–274.

Bloch, V. (1973). Cerebral activation and memory fixation. *Archives de Italiennes Biologie, 111,* 577–590.

Crick, F., & Mitchison, G. (1983). The function of dream sleep. *Nature, 304,* 111–114.

Dement, W. (1955). Dream recall and eye movements during sleep in schizophrenics and normals. *Journal of Nervous and Mental Disease, 122,* 263–269.

Everson, C. A., Gilliland, M. A., Kushida, C. A., Pilcher, J. J., Fang, V. S., Refetoff, S., Bergmann, B. M., & Rechtschaffen, A. (1989). Sleep deprivation in the rat: IX. Recovery. *Sleep, 12,* 60–67.

Fishbein, W., Kastaniotis, C., & Chattman, D. (1974). Paradoxical sleep: Prolonged augmentation following learning. *Brain Research, 79,* 61–77.

Gilliland, M. A., Bergmann, B. M., & Rechtschaffen, A. (1989). Sleep deprivation in the rat: VII. High EEG amplitude sleep deprivation. *Sleep, 12,* 53–59.

Hartley, D. (1801). *Observations on man, his frame, his duty and his expectations.* London: Johnson.

Heller, C. G., Glotzbach, S., Grahn, D. & Radehe, C. (1988). Sleep dependent changes in the thermo-regulatory system. In R. Lydic & J. F. Biebuyck (Eds) *Clinical physiology of sleep* (pp. 145–158). Bethesda, MD: American Physiological Society.

Hobson, J. A. (1988). *The dreaming brain.* New York: Basic Books.

Hobson, J. A. (1989). *Sleep.* New York: Scientific American Library.

Hobson, J. A., Lydic, R., & Baghdoyan, H. A. (1986). Evolving concepts of sleep generation: From brain centers to neuronal populations (with commentaries). *Behavioral and Brain Sciences, 9,* 371–448.

Jouvet, M. (1962). Récherche sur les structures nerveuses et les mécanismes responsables des differentes phases du sommeil physiologique. *Archives de Italiennes Biologie, 100,* 125–206.

Jouvet, M. (1972). The role of monoamines and acetylcholine-containing neurons in the regulation of the sleep-waking cycle. *Ergebn. Physiology Biol. Chem. Exp. Pharmakol., 64,* 166–307.

Jouvet, M., Buda, L., Denges, M., Kitahama, K., Sallanon, M., & Sastre, J. (1988). Hypothalamic regulation of paradoxical sleep. In T. Onian (Ed.) *Neurobiology of sleep–wakefulness cycle* (pp. 1–17). Metsniereba, Tbilisi: Georgian Academy of Sciences.

Karczmar, A. G., Longo, V. G., & De Carolis, A. S. (1970). A pharmacological model of paradoxical sleep: The role of cholinergic and monoamine systems. *Physiological Behavior, 5,* 175–182.

Krueger, J. M., Walter, J., Dinarello, C. A., & Chedid, L. (1985a). Induction of slow-wave sleep by interleukin-1. In M. J. Kluger, J. J. Oppenheim, & M. C. Powanda (Eds) *The physiologic, metabolic and immunologic actions of interleukin-1* (pp. 161–170). New York: Liss.

Krueger, J. M., Walter, J., & Levin, C. (1985b). Factor S and related somnogens: An immune theory for slow-wave sleep. In D. J. McGinty, R. Drucker-Colin, A. Morrison, & P. L. Parmeggiani (Eds) *Brain mechanisms of sleep* (pp. 253–275). New York: Raven.

Kushida, C. A., Bergmann, B. M., & Rechtschaffen, R. (1989). Sleep deprivation in the rat: IV. Paradoxical sleep deprivation. *Sleep, 12,* 22–30.

Luria, A. R. (1968). *The mind of a mnemonist.* Cambridge, MA: Harvard University Press.

Mikulincer, M., Babkoff, H., Caspy, T., & Sing, H. (1989). The effects of 72 hours of sleep loss on psychological variables. *British Journal of Psychology, 80,* 145–162.

Moore-Ede, M. C., Czeisler, C. A., & Richardson, G. S. (1983). Circadian timekeeping in health and disease. *New England Journal of Medicine, 309,* 469–476.

Moruzzi, G. (1972). The sleep–waking cycle. *Ergeb. Physiol. Biol. Chem. Exp. Pharmakol., 64,* 1–165.

Pappenheimer, J. R., Koski, G., Fenci, V., Karnovsky, M. L., & Krueger, J. (1975). Extraction of sleep-promoting factor S from cerebrospinal fluid and from brain of sleep-deprived animals. *Journal of Neurophysiology, 38,* 1299–1311.

Parmeggiani, P. L. (1988). Thermoregulation during sleep from the viewpoint of homeostasis. In R. Lydic & J. F. Biebuyck (Eds) *Clinical physiology of sleep* (pp. 159–170). Bethesda, MD: American Physiological Society.

Pavlov, I. P. (1960). *Conditioned reflexes: An investigation of the physiological activity of the cerebral cortex* (G. V. Anrep, trans.). New York: Dover.

Rechtschaffen, A., Bergmann, B. M., Everson, C. A., Kushida, C. A., & Gilliland, M. A. (1989a). Sleep deprivation in the rat: I. Conceptual issues. *Sleep, 12,* 1–4.

Rechtschaffen, A., Bergmann, B. M., Everson, C. A., Kushida, C. A., & Gilliland, M. A. (1989b). Sleep deprivation in the rat: X. Integration and discussion of the findings. *Sleep, 12,* 68–87.

Roffwarg, H. P., Muzio, J. M., & Dement, W. C. (1966). Ontogenetic development of the human sleep–dream cycle. *Science, 152,* 604–619.

Sherrington, C. (1955). *Man on his nature.* New York: Doubleday.

Silverman, D. H. S., & Karnovsky, M. L. (1989). Serotonin and peptide neuro-modulators: Recent disorders and new ideas. In A. Meister (Ed.) *Advances in enzymology.* New York: Wiley.

Smith, C., & Lapp, L. (1986). Prolonged increases in both PS and number of REMs following a shuttle avoidance task. *Physiological Behavior, 36*(6), 1053–1057.

Smith, C., Kitahama, K., Valatx, J. L., & Jouvet, M. (1974). Increased paradoxical sleep in mice during acquisition of a shock avoidance task. *Brain Research, 77,* 221–230.

Smith, C., Young, J., & Young, W. (1980). Prolonged increases in paradoxical sleep during and after avoidance-task acquisition. *Sleep, 3*(1), 67–81.

Steraide, M., & Hobson, J. A. (1976). Neuronal activity during the sleep–waking cycle. *Progress in Neurobiology, 6,* 155–376.

5

PSYCHOPHARMACOLOGY

Leonard W. Hamilton and C. Robin Timmons

Rutgers University, New Jersey, USA

The human experience is frequently characterized by our feelings towards certain aspects of our environment. We are frightened by things we do not understand, calmed by familiarity, anxious in the face of uncertainty, exhilarated by our accomplishments, and depressed by our losses. Gradually, over the course of our individual development, we come to expect certain situations to produce certain types of feelings.

There are many chemical substances that have the power to alter this relationship between environment and feeling. Anxiety can be transformed into tranquillity, exhilaration into sobriety, and torpor into vigour. When these substances are administered in a formal manner, they are called *drugs*, and the study of the effects of these drugs on mood and other behaviours defines the field of *psychopharmacology*.

Historically, the more common chemical substances that change behaviour were plant products that were widely available and self-administered. Tea and opium were available in the Orient; tobacco and coffee in the Americas; and alcohol throughout the world. The substances were valued by each culture for the effects that they had on behaviour, but each culture also developed written or unwritten guidelines to regulate the use of the substances.

In addition to the commonly available plants, each geographic region has more obscure plants that may contain psychologically active substances. Information about the identifying features and effectiveness of these plants was passed on to family elders and to religious leaders. These individuals became valued for their knowledge of the effects of chemical substances, and became the informal practitioners of *folk medicine*. This gave way to the development of still more knowledge of these effects, and to the gradual development of formal medical practitioners.

We now have literally hundreds of different drugs that are known to change behaviour. Some of these have been borrowed directly from folk medicine and simply represent the modern processing and reformulation of a drug application that may be centuries old. Others have been discovered by accident when a chemical reaction has gone awry or when a drug has been administered to treat one malady and it ends up being effective for some totally different problem. Although important contributions have been made from both of these sources, the vast majority of our modern drugs have been developed through systematic research on the relationships among drugs, behaviour, and the underlying chemistry of the brain.

CLASSIFICATION OF PSYCHOACTIVE DRUGS

Psychoactive drugs have two basic uses: to alter mood and states of consciousness, and to treat psychopathology. Table 1 lists some examples of each type of drug.

Drugs that are used to alter moods and general states of consciousness can be divided into three broad categories based on the type of change they produce in the nervous system. Stimulant drugs produce an exaggeration of the conditions that are normally associated with alert wakefulness; in high dosages, these drugs produce overt seizure activity. Depressant drugs produce an exaggeration of the conditions that are normally associated with relaxation and sleep; in high dosages these drugs can produce unconsciousness. Hallucinogens produce a distortion of normal perception and thought processes; in high dosages these drugs can produce episodes of behaviour that can be characterized as psychotic. Although there are exceptions, a general rule is that these drugs produce their effects rather immediately by direct action on the neurons of the brain.

Table 1 Psychoactive drugs

Drug class	Example drugs	Primary mechanism of action
Drugs used to alter moods and states of consciousness		
STIMULANTS (produce psychomotor arousal; treat attention deficit disorder)		
Sympathomimetics	Dextroamphetamine	Monoamine (DA & NE) agonist,
	Methylphenidate	increase release, block re-uptake
	Cocaine	
Cholinomimetics	Nicotine	Ach agonist (high dose blocks)
Xanthines	Caffeine	Block adenosine receptors, GABA antagonist
Convulsants	Strychnine	Glycine antagonist
DEPRESSANTS (produce sedation; treat pain, anxiety, sleep disorders)		
Opioids	Morphine, Codeine	Endogenous opiate agonist
	Heroin, Methadone	
Barbiturates	Secobarbital	GABA agonist
Barbiturate-like	Meprobamate	Similar to Barbiturates
Organic solvents	Alcohol, Ether	Disrupt neuronal membrane; may facilitate GABA
HALLUCINOGENIC (produce distorted perception)		
NE-like	Mescaline	Alter 5HT activity
5HT-like	Lysergic acid diethylamide (LSD)	Alter 5HT activity
Other	Marijuana, Anti-cholinergics, Phencyclidine (PCP)	Varied mechanisms, but many have endogenous receptors
Drugs used to treat psychological disorders		
ANTIPSYCHOTICS (treat schizophrenia; also delirium and dementia)		
Phenothiazines	Chlorpromazine	Block DA receptors
Butyrophenones	Haloperidol	Block DA receptors
Other	Clozapine	Block DA receptors
ANTIDEPRESSANTS (treat depression and bipolar disorder)		
Tricyclics		Block NE and 5HT re-uptake
(secondary)	Nortriptyline	(primarily block NE)
(tertiary)	Imipramine	(primarily block 5HT)
	Clomipramine	
Heterocyclics	Fluoxetine	Block NE and 5HT re-uptake
MAO inhibitors	Phenelzine	Inhibit monoamine oxidase
	Tranylcypromine	
Lithium	Lithium	Stabilizes synapses
ANTI-ANXIETY (treat acute and chronic anxiety; also sleep disturbances)		
Benzodiazepines	Alprazolam	Facilitate GABA
	Diazepam	
Other	Buspirone	Decrease 5HT activity

Notes: Ach = acetylcholine
   DA = dopamine
   5HT = 5-hydroxytryptamine
   GABA = gamma amino butyric acid
   MAO = monoamine oxidase
   NE = norepinephrine (noradrenaline)

Drugs that are used to treat psychopathology can also be divided into three broad categories based on the types of symptoms that they can ameliorate. The anti-anxiety drugs are used to treat the day-to-day fears and anxieties of individuals who lead basically normal lives. The antidepressant drugs are used to treat feelings of negative affect that may range from mild melancholy to abject depression accompanied by suicidal tendencies. Finally, the antipyschotic drugs are used to treat severe forms of mental illness, most notably schizophrenia, in which patients lose contact with reality and engage in behaviours that fall considerably outside the realm of normality. Again, there are exceptions, but a general rule is that these drugs tend to act indirectly: although they have immediate effects on the neurons of the brain, the therapeutic effects often require several weeks to appear, suggesting that the behavioural changes must await some long-term, chronic adjustment of the neurons to the drug's actions (i.e., *neuromodulation*).

There are many drugs that are not listed in the general classification schema of Table 1. Such a table can never remain complete for very long because new drugs are continually being developed, new applications may be found for some drugs, old drugs are sometimes phased out of the market-place, and new theory may change the boundaries of classification. Detailed and current information that would expand this table is compiled regularly and published in a variety of sources (e.g., *Goodman and Gilman's The Pharmacological Bases of Therapeutics* and the *Physicians' Desk Reference*). Paperback summaries of this information for prescription and non-prescription drugs are available from bookshops and libraries. We shall return to Table 1 later for a discussion of the mechanisms of actions for these drugs.

SOME PRINCIPLES OF PHARMACOLOGY

In order for a drug to have an effect on behaviour, it must come into contact with the appropriate neurons in the brain. This can be accomplished in numerous ways, and the decision about the route of administration is based on a combination of factors including convenience, effects of the drug on local tissue, solubility of the drug, ionic characteristics of the drug, size of the drug molecule, and vulnerability of the drug to metabolism. The most common mode of administration is *oral*, with the drug being absorbed into the bloodstream through the walls of the stomach and intestines. *Sub-cutaneous*, *transdermal*, and *intramuscular* routes tend to produce slower and more sustained rates of delivery. *Inhalation* of drug vapours or injection of drugs directly into the bloodstream (*intra-arterial* or *intravenous*) tend to produce very rapid onset of the drug effects. Minute quantities of drugs can be injected directly into the brain (*intracranial*) or into the spinal cord (*intrathecal*) to produce rapid effects that are restricted to the local area of injection.

The duration of drug action is determined primarily by the rate of metabolic inactivation of the drug. Most commonly, the drugs are metabolized into some inactive form by enzymes that are produced by the liver, the digestive tract, or by the nervous system tissue per se. These drug metabolites are removed from the body as waste products in the bowel, in the urine, through the skin, or by exhalation through the lungs. Drugs can sometimes be present in the body but have little or no effect because the drug molecules have been sequestered into a metabolically inactive *pool*. Examples of such pools include the bladder, fat deposits, or chemical bonding of drug molecules to larger protein molecules.

The relationship between the dosage of a drug and the response to that drug poses one of the thorniest problems in psychopharmacology. Common experience can provide a general description of the dose–response effect: for example, a sip of coffee will be subthreshold and will not help a student stay awake to study; a cupful will certainly help, and two might be better; five or six cups might lead to tremor and anxiety. These different responses to caffeine reflect the different concentrations of the drug in the blood. Technically, the lowest dose required to produce the desired effect (in 50 per cent of the subjects) is termed the *minimum effective dose* (MED-50), and a dosage that is lethal to 50 per cent of the subjects (the LD-50) is an index of the toxicity of the drug. The safety factor of a drug, the *therapeutic index*, is the ratio of LD-50/MED-50, which should be a large number (10 or more) to indicate that a *lethal dose* would be many times higher than the recommended dose.

Within the effective dose range, the responses may still be complicated. Typically, doubling the dosage does not double the effect, and many drugs show a bipolar *dose–response curve* as shown in Figure 1. In the case of caffeine, for example, moderate doses can enhance typing skills but heavier doses begin to increase the number of errors. Furthermore, on tasks that are not well practised, even low doses may impair performance; the dose–response relationship is determined as much by the details of the response as the details of the drug's biochemistry.

The effects of a particular drug dosage also depend on the condition of the subject when the drug is administered. The *law of initial values* is an old concept that was first formulated to describe the effects of drugs on the cardiovascular system. Some drugs, for example, may be very effective in lowering blood pressure, but only if the blood pressure is abnormally high to begin with. This concept applies equally well in psychopharmacology, and is frequently referred to as the *rate–dependency* effect. Individuals who are already highly aroused may respond adversely to even small doses of a stimulant drug because it effectively increases the arousal to a level that interferes with performance. Similarly, many drugs that have antidepressant or antianxiety effects may produce relatively little change in the mood of individuals who are not suffering from depression or anxiety.

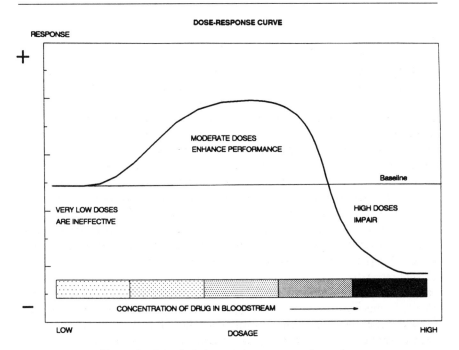

Figure 1 A typical dose–response curve for a drug

A particularly interesting drug effect is one that can occur when the dosage is zero. The *placebo* effect (placebo is Latin for "I will please") occurs when an inactive substance such as saline or a sugar capsule is represented as a drug, and leads to the relief of symptoms. This does not necessarily mean that either the initial symptoms or the relief of symptoms was imaginary. In the case of pain relief, for example, it is now clear that placebo effects are the result of the body's release of endogenous opiates in response to the belief that a drug was given. This type of behavioural effect is almost certainly a regular occurrence that increases or decreases the impact of real drug effects.

Given the intricate nature of the dose–response relationship, it should come as no surprise that subject variables play an important role. From childhood through senescence, there occur systematic changes in metabolism, body weight, and neurochemistry which can alter the effects of drugs. Hormonal differences between males and females, systematic differences in certain enzymes, and even cultural and climatic differences can further alter the effects of drugs. Finally, the individual's history of drug use may also produce long-term changes in metabolism of certain drugs that can either reduce their effectiveness (*tolerance*) or, less commonly, increase their effectiveness (*sensitization*). These contributing factors rarely appear on the labels of either prescription or non-prescription drugs, but should always be considered for patients who do not represent a typical category.

Drugs are not magic bullets: even under the most carefully controlled conditions, a particular drug can influence either multiple neurotransmitter systems or multiple systems that use the same neurotransmitter. The pattern of this combination of effects can change with drug dosage. As a result, drugs frequently have undesirable *side-effects*, but these complications may diminish with time or be controlled by adjusting the drug dosage. In many cases, the side-effects of the drug may mimic the symptoms of some other disorder, for example, a drug that successfully treats depression might cause anxiety. The existence of side-effects simply means that the effects of the drug on the brain are influencing pathways that are not specifically a part of the problem that was diagnosed.

The utility of any particular drug or elixir can be determined empirically. The successful treatment of previous patients can provide information about the most appropriate route of administration and dosage to use and the types of side-effects to watch for. For example, if it is observed that alcohol can reduce anxiety, the clinician might suggest that the anxious patient have a glass of wine with dinner. These types of observations and decisions have been useful in the development of folk medicines, but modern pharmacology relies more heavily on theory and mechanism. The development of a new and better drug treatment requires an understanding of both the disease process (i.e., the brain structures that are dysfunctional) and the way in which the drug alters this process (i.e., the neurochemical actions of the drug.) We turn now to a discussion of these mechanisms.

MECHANISMS OF DRUG ACTION IN THE BRAIN

One of the most elegant experiments in the history of pharmacology was performed in the mid-nineteenth century by a French physiologist, Claude Bernard (1813–1878). Explorers had brought back *curare*, a compound that native South Americans used as a poison on their blowgun darts to paralyse large mammals. Bernard was able to demonstrate that curare did not influence either the nerve fibres or the muscle fibres, but rather acted at the junction between these two structures (Bernard & Pelouze, 1850).

Several decades later, the English physiologist, Sir Charles S. Sherrington (1857–1952) studied the special properties of the junction between one neuron and the next, and coined the term *synapse* to label this gap (Sherrington, 1897). He observed that the transmission of messages through the synapse differed in several ways from electric transmission through the nerve fibre: (1) messages passed in only one direction, (2) messages were changed as they travelled through the synapse, (3) messages were delayed at the synapse by 0.5 millisecond, and (4) some messages inhibited other messages. Knowledge of electricity was still in its infancy, but it was known that electric signals could not mimic these features of the synapse.

At the beginning of the twentieth century, several researchers began to suspect that the transmission of messages across the synapse might involve chemicals. Many chemicals were known to influence the activity of the nervous system, and some of these (e.g., *acetylcholine* and *noradrenaline*) were present in the body. Although these chemicals could influence neuronal activity in laboratory preparations, there was no proof that they served as messengers under normal circumstances. The method of proof finally came to one of the researchers in a dream, and the German-American biochemist Otto Loewi (1873–1961) went into his laboratory on Easter Sunday in 1921 to perform the critical experiment.

Loewi's experiment was elegant and simple (Loewi, 1921). He dissected one frog's heart with a portion of the vagus nerve attached, a second heart without the vagus nerve, and placed them into separate containers of saline. Both hearts continued beating and, as expected from previous observations, electric stimulation of the vagus nerve caused the beating of the first heart to slow down. The clever part of the experiment was the pumping of the saline from the first beaker into the second. When this was done, the second heart also slowed down when the vagus nerve of the first heart was stimulated. There was no electric connection between the two hearts, and the only possible way that the message could be transmitted from one to the other was through the release of a chemical messenger into the surrounding fluid. Loewi dubbed the substance *Vagusstoff* (which turned out to be acetylcholine) and was later awarded the Nobel Prize for this first demonstration of the *chemical transmission* of neural messages.

Chemical messages could account for the special properties of the synapse observed by Sherrington (1897). The release of a chemical messenger by one neuron on to the next would restrict the flow of information to one direction. Specific types of chemical messengers might be expected to inhibit rather than excite the next neuron. The chemical message would not be expected to maintain the specific temporal features of the volley of impulses that caused its release. Finally, the time required for the release and delivery of the chemical message could easily account for the 0.5-millisecond delay that Sherrington had observed. Despite all of these explanations, it still required a bold imagination in the 1920s to believe that tiny neurons could release several hundred chemical messages per second to conduct the complex functions of the nervous system.

Because of its accessibility and known functions, the peripheral autonomic nervous system became the natural choice as a test system for studying chemical transmission. Following Loewi's experiment, it soon became apparent that acetylcholine served as a chemical messenger in several locations. It was released not only on to the heart muscle by the vagus nerve, but also on to the smooth muscles of all the organs and glands served by the parasympathetic system. Furthermore, acetylcholine was the messenger at the synapses in both the sympathetic and parasympathetic ganglia. It was also the messenger at the nerve—muscle junction for the striated muscles of voluntary movement (where the receptors can be blocked by curare, as in Bernard's experiment). But it became clear that acetylcholine was not the only neurotransmitter. Some other substance was being released on to the smooth muscles by the fibres of the sympathetic system, and that substance was determined to be noradrenaline, a substance very closely related to adrenaline, the hormone of the adrenal gland.

Now, the logic and the power of chemical transmission began to unfold. When different systems were anatomically separate as in the case of the separate locations of the sympathetic and parasympathetic ganglia, the same neurotransmitter could be used without confusion. But when two opposing systems projected to the same organ, for example the heart, then the release of different chemical messengers (e.g., acetylcholine to slow the heartbeat; noradrenaline to speed the heartbeat) could determine the different functions. But the autonomic nervous system was not going to yield all of the answers this simply.

A particular transmitter substance did not always produce the same effect. In the case of acetylcholine, there were two *receptor* types, *muscarinic* and *nicotinic*, which responded to different aspects of the molecule. Similarly, in the case of noradrenaline, there were also two receptor types, termed *alpha* and *beta*. The early researchers were eager to categorize these different receptor types into functional categories. The initial suspicions that acetylcholine was always inhibitory and noradrenaline was always excitatory had already been disconfirmed. The discovery of different receptor types for each compound held the possibility that these could be classified as excitatory or inhibitory. But it was not to be — the specific receptor type is strictly for encoding the arrival of a message, and that message can be used as either a signal for excitation or inhibition.

While the details of chemical transmission were unfolding, other brain researchers had sought to relate anatomic structures of the brain to specific behavioural functions. Considerable progress was made in this effort, and research continues to sharpen the structure—function relationships. However, the discovery of chemical transmission required that yet another layer of organization be added — neurons within a particular anatomic structure could have different neurotransmitters.

One of the clearest examples of this was a set of experiments done by S. P. Grossman in 1960. Previous research had demonstrated that lesions of the lateral hypothalamus produced a dramatic reduction in both eating and drinking, whereas electric stimulation elicited both eating and drinking. Grossman was able to separate these functions by applying different chemicals directly into the lateral hypothalamus through a chronically implanted cannula. Drugs that mimic acetylcholine elicited drinking only, whereas drugs that mimic noradrenaline elicited eating only. Drugs that block acetylcholine receptors reduced drinking in thirsty rats, whereas drugs that block noradrenaline receptors reduced eating in hungry rats. These results provided a finer grained analysis than the experiments that were based strictly on anatomy. Within the anatomic boundaries of the lateral hypothalamus are chemically coded functions for eating (noradrenergic) and drinking (cholinergic).

Given the knowledge that chemical coding at synapses is superimposed on anatomic subdivisions, we can now begin to understand how drugs can produce their specific effects on behaviour. The third column of Table 1 describes the action of the drug at the level of the individual neuron or synapse as illustrated in Figure 2. As more of the blanks in this table are filled, we gain a better understanding of the relationship between behaviour and its underlying pharmacologic bases. Drugs can be classified, for example, as *mimickers* of neurotransmitters, *blockers* of receptors, *facilitators* of neurotransmitter release, *presynaptic blockers* of activity, *inhibitors* of specific enzymes, and so forth. The list of neurotransmitters grew slowly at first

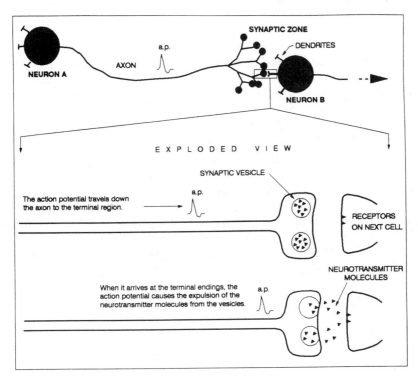

Figure 2 Major steps in the process of chemical transmission

Table 2 Some of the many neurotransmitters

Acetylcholine	Peptides (several dozen)
Serotonin	Enkephalins (opiate-like)
Adrenaline	Leu-enkephalin
Dopamine	Met-enkephalin
Noradrenaline	
Amino acids	GABA
Aspartate	Histamine
Glycine	Carbon monoxide
Glutamate	Nitric oxide
Others	Others

Note: GABA = gamma amino butyric acid

(acetylcholine, noradrenaline, dopamine), but since the early 1980s the list has exploded to more than 100 different chemicals (see Table 2).

Drugs that influence behaviour must do so by influencing the brain, and there are several features of the brain that have contributed to a widespread misunderstanding of its basic character. Neurons, unlike most other cells, do not undergo cell division, so the brain contains virtually all of its cells at the time of birth. These cells are already committed to the general *structure–function relationships* that are seen in the adult brain, thus encouraging the view of the brain as a stable, organized set of neural circuits with individual experiences simply selecting different combinations of existing pathways; not unlike the structure of a computer (the hardware) that can be used for a host of different functions (the software).

This view of the brain as a static set of complex circuits is wrong. Although the general features and structure–function relationships are fixed, the details of neuronal actions are dynamic and constantly changing. When certain activity in the brain acts repeatedly to produce some behaviour, the circuits that are active can undergo physical changes (e.g., increased production of neurotransmitter molecules, expansion of the branching terminals of the axons, increased complexity of the receiving dendritic tree, increased number of receptors, etc.) which result in the enhanced efficiency of the system. The behaviour that is produced can produce changes in the environment, and changes in the environment (whether mediated by behaviour or not) can, in turn, produce changes in the brain.

A good way to conceptualize this (see Figure 3) is to view the brain, behaviour, and the environment as an interacting triangle, with each dimension influencing the other two (cf. Hamilton & Timmons, 1990). These interpenetrating effects require a more complex view of the results of various experimental manipulations. Although a particular drug may produce a very specific change in behaviour, we must not fall into the trap of viewing this as a singular effect. The neuronal systems that were directly influenced by the

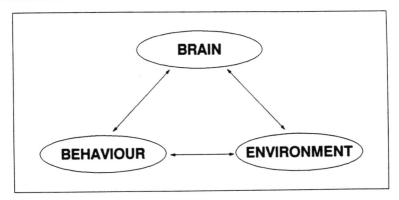

Figure 3 The brain, behaviour, and environment interact continually, and each changes the other two

drug will also undergo a longer-term change as a result of the drug's presence (and absence). The resulting behaviour will change the environment and that change will change other aspects of behaviour, and so forth. An appreciation of this dynamic interaction helps to provide a more complete understanding of the effects of drugs on behaviour.

The discipline of psychopharmacology in its modern form arose from the convergence of two separate areas of study: first, the growing information about neurotransmission and the drugs that influenced it, and second, B. F. Skinner's development of *operant conditioning* techniques for the study of behaviour. Skinner's methodology (e.g., Reynolds, 1975) provided powerful methods for analysing behavioural change, and numerous animal models began to emerge for the screening of potentially useful drugs. The antipsychotic drugs rather specifically interfered with conditioned emotional responses, anti-anxiety drugs blocked the normal response to punishment, stimulant and depressant drugs changed general levels of activity, and so forth. The efficiency of these procedures greatly facilitated the accumulation of knowledge about the effects of drugs on behaviour, and became an indispensable link in the pathway of drugs from the chemist's bench to the pharmacist's shelf.

MECHANISMS OF DRUG ACTIONS ON BEHAVIOUR

Drugs that alter moods and states of consciousness

Central nervous system stimulants

Drugs can be classified as stimulants based on their ability to produce behavioural arousal, characteristic patterns of electroencephalographic

(EEG) arousal, increases in motor activity, or some combination of these. These changes can be accomplished by several different mechanisms of action.

The so-called convulsant drugs such as *strychnine, picrotoxin*, and *pentylenetetrazol* are representative of the different modes of action. Strychnine blocks the receptors for *glycine*, an inhibitory neurotransmitter. Picrotoxin reduces chloride permeability through its actions on the *GABA receptor complex*. (Gamma amino butyric acid, or GABA, is the most widespread neurotransmitter in the brain.) Pentylenetetrazol decreases the recovery time between action potentials by increasing potassium permeability of the axon. Drugs such as *caffeine, theophylline*, and *theobromine* (present in coffee, tea, and chocolate) stimulate the activity of neurons by increasing the calcium permeability of membranes. Note that all of these drugs produce rather general effects that can influence neurons irrespective of the particular neurotransmitter system, and the state induced by these drugs is sometimes referred to as *non-specific arousal*. In low to moderate dosages they can enhance learning and performance in a wide variety of situations, but with higher dosages, behaviour is impaired and dangerous seizures can be induced.

The *amphetamines* and *cocaine* may be the best-known stimulant drugs, and both categories have rather specific effects on neurons that release dopamine or noradrenaline. Although the effects are not entirely specific, amphetamine stimulates these neurons by promoting the release of these neurotransmitters, while cocaine tends to block their reuptake. The restriction of the drug effects to a certain class of neurons is mirrored by a more specific change in behaviour. Some non-specific arousal can be observed, but these two types of drugs have a profound effect in situations that involve specific behavioural responses that result in reward.

Central nervous system depressants

Drugs that are classified as central nervous system (CNS) depressants appear to act on two major neurotransmitter systems. One of the neurotransmitters of sleep is *serotonin*, and certain drugs that enhance the activity of serotonin can induce drowsiness and sleep. The other important neurotransmitter is *GABA*, and the more common sedative and hypnotic drugs (e.g., the *benzodiazepines, barbiturates*, and *alcohol*) tend to produce their effects by acting on the GABA receptor complex. Acting on a special receptor site, they facilitate the action of GABA and inhibit neuronal activity by increasing the permeability of the neuronal membranes to chloride ions.

The *narcotic* drugs deserve special mention as CNS depressants. Extracts of the opium poppy have been used for thousands of years for both medicinal (pain relief) and recreational (general sense of well-being) effects. *Opium* (a mixture of *morphine* and *codeine*) is naturally occurring, whereas *heroin* is a synthetic drug. The powerful effects of these drugs could not be explained by their actions on any of the known neurotransmitters. Finally, in the 1970s, it was determined that some neurons had specific receptors for these compounds, and that the body produced a variety of different substances (some chemical neurotransmitters and some hormones) that acted like the narcotic drugs. These endogenous morphine-like substances, termed *endorphins*, are released in response to various types of pain or stress.

Hallucinogens

Although drugs that stimulate or depress the general activity of the brain lead to changes in the interaction with the environment, these changes tend to be more quantitative than qualitative. Hallucinogens, on the other hand, produce fundamental changes in the sensorium. Visual and auditory distortions and imagery may be experienced. Tactile sensations may occur without stimulus. In some cases there may occur a conflation of experiences, called synesthesia, in which visual experiences may be "heard" or tactile experiences "seen" in ways that almost never occur in the absence of the drug. The drugs that produce these changes are derived from a variety of different plant sources as well as synthetic sources and tend to produce changes in many different neurotransmitter systems. The mechanism of action that causes the hallucinations remains clouded, but there is a growing consensus that these drugs act on serotonin receptors.

Some observations on abuse and addiction

If a drug is administered repeatedly, there is frequently a reduction in the effectiveness of the drug, called tolerance. This can occur through several different mechanisms: (1) liver enzymes may be induced to speed up drug degradation; (2) presynaptic neurons may increase or decrease the production of neurotransmitters; (3) postsynaptic neurons may increase or decrease the number of receptors; and (4) opposing systems may increase or decrease their activity. Typically, more than one of these countermeasures is launched, and the brain's activity gradually becomes more normalized despite the presence of the drug.

Tolerance sets the stage for another phenomenon. If the drug administration is suddenly stopped, the mechanisms of tolerance are unmasked and *withdrawal symptoms* occur. As a result of the mechanisms of tolerance, the brain functions more normally in the presence of a drug than in its absence.

The types of tolerance described above are referred to as *pharmacological tolerance*. These mechanisms cannot always account for the observed decline in response to the drug. For example, amphetamine reduces the amount of milk that rats will drink during a daily session, but by the tenth day, drinking has returned to normal levels. However, if the drug is administered alone for ten days, and milk is offered on the eleventh day, the drug still suppresses drinking. The return to normal drinking requires learning to perform the behaviour in the presence of the drug. This type of effect is known as *behavioural tolerance* (Carlton & Wolgin, 1971).

The facts that many drugs have direct rewarding effects and that tolerance can develop to these rewarding effects can lead to motivation for *self-administration* of drugs. Drugs that have the capacity to produce such motivation typically share three characteristics: they act on the central nervous system, they act rapidly, and the cessation of use produces withdrawal symptoms. These characteristics can produce an *acquired motivational state* (i.e., a desire or motivation for the effects of the drug) which can lead to addiction or abuse of the drug. The narcotic drugs are among the most potent in this regard.

Just as some individuals may be more sensitive to the effects of a drug because of differences in metabolism, specific neurotransmitter activity, or other subject variables, so might some individuals be more susceptible to acquiring the motivational states that we call addiction or substance abuse. There is growing evidence that this susceptibility may have a genetic basis. In the case of alcohol abuse, for example, there is a clear tendency for sons of alcoholics to be more likely to become alcoholics, and preliminary evidence points to a genetic defect that may alter the response to reward (e.g., Blum, 1991). This and related evidence may soon provide a physiologic basis for the somewhat ill-chosen term, *addictive personality*.

Drugs used to treat disorders of behaviour

Antipsychotics

The discovery of the drugs that are used to treat psychoses (primarily *schizophrenia*) followed a strange and fascinating pathway. A French surgeon, Henri Laborit, was convinced in the 1940s that many of the deaths associated with surgery could be attributed to the patients' own fears about the dangers of surgery (see Palfai & Jankiewicz, 1991, p. 10). Attempts to reduce this distress with sedatives or by blocking the autonomic nervous system were only marginally effective. Laborit concluded that what was needed was a drug that could dissolve the fear response itself – in his words, a Pavlovian deconditioner. His search led to one of the newly developed antihistamine compounds (promethazine), and a variant of this compound, *chlorpromazine*, proved to be dramatically effective. Patients who received this drug pre-surgically were calm, minimally sedated, and the incidence of deaths from surgical shock was greatly reduced.

Soon, of course, the use of chlorpromazine spread to the psychiatric clinic and was found to produce an equally dramatic reversal of the symptoms of schizophrenia. Chlorpromazine and related *phenothiazine* drugs were responsible for the release of hundreds of thousands of patients from institutions where they otherwise would have spent the remainder of their lives in heavy sedation, in strait-jackets, or other restraints. The patients were not cured, but for many, they were able for the first time in years to engage in relatively normal day-to-day interactions.

Laborit's characterization of chlorpromazine as a Pavlovian deconditioner was upheld. In proper doses, the phenothiazines can specifically reduce signalled avoidance responding in animals while not influencing the direct response to an aversive stimulus. More recently, an even more specific animal (and human) model of this disorder has been developed by Jeffrey Gray and his colleagues at the University of London (see Baruch, Hemsley, & Gray, 1988). They view much of the anxiety associated with schizophrenia as being the result of a discordance between current perceptions and perceived regularities of past events. For example, normal individuals who have heard 30 presentations of a bell do not readily acquire a conditional response (sometimes called a conditioned response) if this bell is now paired with electric shock – a phenomenon known as *latent inhibition*. Patients suffering from schizophrenia are impaired in latent inhibition, and this deficit is normalized by chlorpromazine.

These antipsychotic drugs produce a variety of effects on neurons, but almost certainly produce their beneficial effects by blocking the *D2 receptor* for dopamine. When all of the drugs in common clinical use are rank-ordered according to their potency, the rank-ordering is identical to that achieved when they are rank-ordered according to their ability to block the D2 receptor. A similar order is obtained when they are ranked according to their specific ability to inhibit avoidance responding, and given time, there will almost certainly be a similar concordance when rank-ordered in terms of their effects on latent inhibition.

These close relationships between clinically useful drugs, animal models, affinity to specific receptors, and theoretical models of neurotransmitters and behaviour have brought us to a point where it is not unrealistic to suppose that schizophrenia can be understood in the foreseeable future, perhaps even prevented or cured.

Anti-anxiety drugs

The success of chlorpromazine in dissolving the acute fears that surround surgery as well as the pervasive fears that torment the psychotic mind led to the search for milder drugs that could allay more commonplace anxieties. The barbiturate drugs (and alcohol) had been used with some success, but dosages that reduced anxiety also produced troublesome side-effects of sedation. This situation led to the marketing of *meprobamate*, which was claimed to ease anxiety without sedation. This drug became very popular, even though it was in fact just a mild barbiturate that had as many sedative effects as the other drugs in this class.

Although meprobamate did not live up to its initial promise, the claims of specificity did promote the search for other drugs that could have these effects. By the early 1960s two such drugs (*chlordiazepoxide* and *diazepam*) had been discovered. Marketed under the trade names of Librium and Valium, these drugs quickly became the most widely prescribed drugs of their time.

Chlordiazepoxide and related *benzodiazepine* compounds were initially termed minor tranquillizers (as contrasted with the antipsychotics that were known as major tranquillizers), but this terminology fell into disfavour and they are now known simply as anti-anxiety compounds. Nearly all of the compounds in this class act by facilitating the activity of the neurotransmitter GABA. The so-called GABA receptor complex is a complicated structure that has a GABA site, a sedative/convulsant site, and a benzodiazepine site. There is now growing evidence that the brain manufactures its own anti-anxiety compounds that are released during periods of stress.

Antidepressants

Antidepressants are drugs that help to reverse mood states which are characterized by sadness, lack of self-esteem, and general depression. A variety of animal models of this disorder has linked depression to the *monoamines*, especially noradrenaline and serotonin.

The first drugs to be used in the treatment of depression were discovered by accident. Tuberculosis patients who were being treated with a new drug called iproniazid seemed to be enjoying a remarkable recovery, but it was soon learned that while their tuberculosis remained unaffected, their understandable mood of depression was being elevated by the drug. It was later learned that *iproniazid* and related drugs inhibit the activity of an enzyme known as *monoamine oxidase* (MAO), and tend to gradually elevate the level of activity of neurons that utilize dopamine or noradrenaline as neurotransmitters.

The search for better and safer drugs to treat depression led to the discovery of a class of compounds called the *tricyclic antidepressants*, so named because their basic chemical structure includes three carbon rings. Most of these compounds appear to act by blocking the re-uptake of dopamine and noradrenaline, but some of them also block the re-uptake of serotonin, some block serotonin alone, and some have no known effect on any of these systems.

Some patients who suffer from depression also have recurrent episodes of manic behaviour. This disorder, known as *bipolar disorder*, is treated most successfully by the administration of *lithium* salts. Lithium tends to stabilize the neurons, preventing the development of mania that is usually followed by a period of deep depression. The neuronal mechanism remains somewhat mysterious, although recent evidence suggests that lithium blocks the synthesis of a *second messenger*, a neuronal compound that promotes long-term changes in the general capacity for synaptic activity (Lickey & Gordon, 1991, chap. 14).

FUTURE DIRECTIONS

The future of psychopharmacology contains many challenges. Certainly one of the major challenges is to understand the biological bases of substance abuse in sufficient detail to allow the prevention and treatment of these devastating disorders. The foundations for this are already in place: the neurotransmitters and anatomic circuitry of the reward system are known in some detail; the psychology of reward and motivational systems has unravelled many of the behavioural contributions to substance abuse; and genetic studies have begun to demonstrate the possibility of predicting and understanding individual differences in the vulnerability of these systems (Kaplan & Sadock, 1985; Lickey & Gordon, 1991).

A second set of challenges involves the development of more specific drugs ("magic bullets") which can restore the victims of depression, schizophrenia, anxiety, and other disorders to normality. Again, the development of these drugs will require a detailed understanding of the neurotransmitters, specific receptor types, and sophisticated understanding of the behavioural contributions to the disorders.

A third, related set of challenges will be to provide drugs that treat and otherwise modify behaviours that are of day-to-day concern for many people: drugs that can facilitate memory, counteract the effects of ageing on cognitive abilities, normalize food intake, and so forth. Some might claim that the availability of more drugs will serve only to exacerbate the problems that we already face with drug abuse. However, drug use and abuse are as old as humankind, and we can only benefit from a better understanding of the effects of drugs on the brain's control of behaviour.

FURTHER READING

Andreasen, N. C. (1984). *The broken brain: The biological revolution in psychiatry.* New York: Harper & Row.

Hamilton, L. W., & Timmons, C. R. (1990). *Principles of behavioral pharmacology: A biopsychological perspective.* Englewood Cliffs, NJ: Prentice-Hall.

Kalat, J. W. (1992). *Biological psychology* (4th edn). Belmont, CA: Wadsworth.

Lickey, M. E., & Gordon, B. (1991). *Medicine and mental illness.* New York: Freeman.

Snyder, S. H. (1986). *Drugs and the brain.* New York: Scientific American.

REFERENCES

Baruch, I., Hemsley, D. R., & Gray, J. (1988). Differential performance of acute and chronic schizophrenics in the latent inhibition task. *Journal of Nervous and Mental Diseases, 176,* 598–606.

Bernard, C., & Pelouze, T. J. (1850). Recherches sur le curare. *Comptes Rendus Hebdomadaires des Séances de l'Academie des Sciences,* Paris, *31,* 533–537.

Blum, K. (1991). *Alcohol and the addictive brain.* New York: Free Press.

Carlton, P. L., & Wolgin, D. L. (1971). Contingent tolerance to the anorexigenic effects of amphetamine. *Physiology and Behavior, 7,* 221–223.

Gilman, A. G., Goodman, L. S., & Gilman, A. (Eds) (1980). *Goodman and Gilman's the pharmacological basis of therapeutics* (6th edn). New York: Macmillan.

Grossman, S. P. (1960). Eating or drinking elicited by direct adrenergic or cholinergic stimulation of hypothalamus. *Science, 132,* 301–302.

Hamilton, L. W., & Timmons, C. R. (1990). *Principles of behavioral pharmacology: A biopsychological perspective.* Englewood Cliffs, NJ: Prentice-Hall.

Kaplan, H. I., & Sadock, B. J. (Eds) (1985). *Comprehensive textbook of psychiatry.* Baltimore, MD: Williams & Wilkins.

Lickey, M. E., & Gordon, B. (1991). *Medicine and mental illness.* New York: Freeman.

Loewi, O. (1921). Über humorale Übertragbarkeit der Herznervenwirkung. *Pflügers Archiv für die gesamte Physiologie des Menschen und der Tiere, 189,* 239–242.

Palfai, T., & Jankiewicz, H. (1991). *Drugs and human behavior.* Dubuque, IA: Wm C. Brown.

Physicians' desk reference (1992). Oradell, NJ: Medical Economics.

Reynolds, G. S. (1975). *A primer of operant conditioning.* Glenview, IL: Scott, Foresman.

Sherrington, C. S. (1897). The central nervous system. In M. Foster (Ed.) *A text book of physiology* (7th edn, vol. 3). London: Macmillan.

GLOSSARY

This glossary is confined to a selection of frequently used terms that merit explanation or comment. Its informal definitions are intended as practical guides to meanings and usages. The entries are arranged alphabetically, word by word, and numerals are positioned as though they were spelled out.

acetylcholine one of the neurotransmitter (q.v.) substances that play a part in relaying information between neurons (q.v.).

ACh a common abbreviation for acetylcholine (q.v.).

action potential the momentary change in electrical potential that occurs when an impulse is propagated along a neuron (q.v.). Also called nerve impulse.

adaptation 1. in evolutionary theory, some feature of an organism's structure, physiology, or behaviour that solves a problem in its life. **2.** In sensory psychology, a temporary change in the responsiveness of a receptor as a result of an increase or decrease in stimulation. **3.** In social psychology, a general term for any process whereby people adapt their behaviour to fit in with a changed cultural environment.

adrenal glands from the Latin *ad*, to, *renes*, kidneys, a pair of endocrine glands (q.v.), situated just above the kidneys, which secrete adrenalin (epinephrine), noradrenalin (norepinephrine) (qq.v.), and other hormones (q.v.) into the bloodstream.

adrenalin(e) hormone (q.v.) secreted by the adrenal glands (q.v.), causing an increase in blood pressure, release of sugar by the liver, and several other physiological reactions to perceived threat or danger. *See also* antidepressant drugs, endocrine glands, noradrenalin(e).

afferent neurons from the Latin *ad*, to, *ferre*, to carry, neurons (q.v.) that transmit impulses from the sense organs to the central nervous system (CNS) (q.v.). *Cf.* efferent neurons.

allele from the Greek *allel*, one another, one of two or more genes (q.v.) responsible for alternative characteristics of a phenotype (q.v.), for example different eye colours

alpha waves high-amplitude brain waves with frequencies of 8–12 Hz, recorded in an electroencephalogram (q.v.), characteristic of relaxed wakefulness in subjects whose eyes are closed. *Cf.* delta waves.

altruism in social psychology and sociobiology, behaviour that benefits another individual or individuals in terms of safety, monetary or other advantages, or chances of survival and reproduction, at some cost to the benefactor. *See also* reciprocal altruism.

amnesia partial or complete loss of memory. Anterograde amnesia is loss of memory for events following the amnesia-causing trauma, or loss of the ability to form long-term memories for new facts and events; retrograde amnesia is loss of memory for events occurring shortly before the trauma.

111

amphetamine any of a class of commonly abused drugs including Benzedrine, Dexedrine, and Methedrine that act as central nervous system stimulants, suppress appetite, increase heart-rate and blood pressure, and induce euphoria.

amygdala an almond-shaped brain structure in the limbic system (q.v.), involved in emotion and motivation, especially aggression, and memory.

anions negatively charged ions (q.v.) such as chloride involved in synaptic transmission of information. *Cf.* cations.

anterograde amnesia *see under* amnesia.

anti-anxiety drugs an umbrella term for a number of drugs, including the benzodiazepine drugs (q.v.) and the muscle relaxant meprobamate, that are used for reducing anxiety, also sometimes called minor tranquillizers.

antidepressant drugs drugs that influence neurotransmitters (q.v.) in the brain, used in the treatment of mood disorders (q. v.), especially depression (q.v.). The monoamine oxidase inhibitor (MAOI) drugs block the absorption of amines such as dopamine, adrenalin, and noradrenalin (qq.v.), allowing these stimulants to accumulate at the synapses in the brain, the tricyclic antidepressants such as imipramine act by blocking the re-uptake of noradrenalin in particular, thereby similarly increasing its availability, and the selective serotonin re-uptake inhibitor fluoxetine hydrochloride (Prozac) blocks the re-uptake of serotonin (q.v.).

antipsychotic drugs a general term for all drugs used to alleviate the symptoms of psychosis (q.v.). Major tranquillizers, including especially the phenothiazine derivatives such as chlorpromazine (Largactil) and thioridazine, are used primarily in the treatment of schizophrenia and other disorders involving psychotic symptoms; lithium compounds are used primarily in the treatment of bipolar (manic-depressive) disorder.

anxiety disorders a group of mental disorders (q.v.) in which anxiety is an important symptom. *See also* obsessive-compulsive disorder, panic disorder, phobia.

anxiolytic drugs another name for anti-anxiety drugs (q.v.).

aphasia loss of language abilities, whether partial or complete, invariably due to an organic brain lesion. There are many forms of aphasia, depending largely on the site of the lesion.

association areas parts of the cerebral cortex (q.v.) not primarily devoted to sensory or motor functions.

autonomic nervous system a subdivision of the nervous system (q.v.) that regulates (autonomously) the internal organs and glands. It is divided into the sympathetic nervous system and the parasympathetic nervous system (qq.v.).

axon from the Greek word meaning axis, a process or extending fibre of a neuron (q.v.) which conducts impulses away from the cell body (q.v.) and transmits them to other neurons.

barbiturates chemical compounds derived from barbituric acid, including barbitone and phenobarbitone, used as hypnotic or sedative drugs, liable to cause strong dependence when abused.

behaviour genetics an interdisciplinary field of study concerned with the genetic or hereditary bases of animal and human behaviour.

behavioural ecology a branch of psychology devoted to understanding behaviour in terms of natural selection (q.v.) and adaptation.

benzodiazepine drugs any of a group of chemical compounds that are used as anti-anxiety drugs (q.v.) and hypnotics (sleeping drugs), including diazepam (Valium) and chlordiazepoxide (Librium).

biological rhythm any periodic, more-or-less regular fluctuation in a biological system controlled by a biological clock, for example a circadian rhythm (q.v.). Biological rhythms should not be confused with the pseudo-scientific doctrine of biorhythms according to which the interaction of three perfectly periodic rhythms, fixed at the time of birth, determine 'good' and 'bad' days throughout life.

bipolar cell a neuron (q.v.), usually a sensory nerve cell, with two processes, axon and dendrite, extending in opposite directions from the cell body.

bipolar disorder a mood disorder (q.v.) in which depression alternates with mania, also known as manic-depressive psychosis.

blood-brain barrier a complex physiological mechanism whose function is to allow blood to flow freely to the brain but to prevent some chemicals present in the blood from reaching the brain.

CAT (computerized axial tomography) *see under* CT (computerized tomography).

catecholamine any member of the group of hormones (q.v.) that are catechol derivatives, especially adrenalin, noradrenalin, and dopamine, (qq.v.), all of which are involved in the functioning of the nervous system (q.v.).

cations positively charges ions (q.v.) such as sodium, potassium, and calcium invoved in synaptic transmission of information. *Cf.* anions.

cell body sometimes called the *soma*, the central part of a neuron (q.v.), containing the nucleus and other structures that keep the cell alive.

central limit theorem in statistics, a theorem showing (roughly) that the sum of any large number of unrelated variables tends to be distributed according to the normal distribution (q.v.). It explains why psychological and biological variables that are due to the additive effects of numerous independently acting causes are distributed approximately normally.

central nervous system (CNS) in human beings and other vertebrates, the brain and spinal cord.

cerebellum from the Latin diminutive form of *cerebrum*, brain, one of the main divisions of the brain, situated beneath the back of the main part of the brain, involved in the regulation of movement and balance.

cerebral cortex from the Latin *cerebrum*, brain, *cortex*, bark, the thin layer of cells covering the cerebrum (q.v.), largely responsible for higher mental functions.

cerebral hemispheres the two halves of the cerebrum (q.v.), which have slightly different functions in human beings.

cerebrum from the Latin word meaning brain, the largest brain structure, comprising the front and upper part of the brain, of which the cortex (outer layer) controls most sensory, motor, and cognitive processes in human beings.

chlordiazepoxide one of the benzodiazepine drugs (q.v.), commonly called Librium.

chromosomes from the Greek *chroma*, colour, *soma*, body, so called because they stain deeply with basic dyes, the microscopic rod-shaped structures in the nucleus of every cell containing deoxyribonucleic acid (DNA) (q.v.) which carries the genes (q.v.) that determine hereditary characteristics. There are 46 chromosomes in every human body cell, apart from the sex cells which carry 23 each.

circadian rhythm from the Latin *circa*, about, *diem*, day, any biological rhythm with a period (from peak to peak or trough to trough) of about 24 hours, including the sleep-wake cycle and other metabolic and physiological processes in human beings.

CNS *see* central nervous system (CNS).

compulsions repetitive, ritualised, stereotyped actions, such as hand-washing, that a person feels unable to stop performing in spite of realizing that the behaviour is inappropriate or excessive, often associated with obsessions (q.v.).

concordance rate in the study of behaviour genetics (q.v.), the proportion of identical twins (or other relatives of known degrees of genetic relatedness) who display the same characteristic or phenotype (q.v.).

consanguinity study in behaviour genetics (q.v.), a comparison of the correlations (q.v.) between pairs of relatives of different known degrees of genetic relatedness on a measurable trait in order to estimate the heritability (q.v.) of the trait. It is also called a family study or a kinship study.

control group in experimental design, a comparison group of subjects who, when the independent variable is manipulated, are not exposed to the treatment that subjects in the experimental group are exposed to, but who in other respects are treated identically to the experimental group, to provide a baseline against which to evaluate the effects of the treatment.

corpus callosum from the Latin *corpus*, body, *callosum*, callous, the band of white fibres that connects the left and right cerebral hemispheres of the brain.

correlation in statistics, the relationship between two variables such that high scores on one tend to go with high scores on the other or (in the case of negative correlation) such that high scores on one tend to go with low scores on the other. The usual index of correlation, called the product-moment correlation coefficient and symbolized by r, ranges from 1.00 for perfect positive correlation, through zero for uncorrelated variables, to -1.00 for perfect negative correlation.

correlational study a non-experimental type of research design in which patterns of correlations (q.v.) are analysed.

critical period a biologically determined stage of development at which a person or animal is optimally ready to acquire some pattern of behaviour. *See also* imprinting.

CT (computerized tomography) a non-invasive method of scanning the brain or other body organ by means of an X-ray beam passed through it repeatedly from different angles, enabling a computer to build up a visual picture, formerly called a CAT (computerized axial tomography) scan. Tomography, from the Greek *tome*, a cutting, is any of a number of techniques used to obtain images of selected plane sections of the human body or other solid objects. *Cf.* magnetic resonance imaging (MRI), PET (positron emission tomography).

DA a common abbreviation for dopamine (q.v.).

delta waves low frequency (1–3 Hz), high amplitude (approximately 150 microvolts) brain waves, recorded on an electroencephalogram (q.v.), characteristic of deep, dreamless sleep. *Cf.* alpha waves.

delusion a false personal belief, maintained in the face of overwhelming contradictory evidence, excluding religious beliefs that are widely accepted by members of the person's culture or sub-culture, characteristic especially of delusional (paranoid) disorder (q.v.). *Cf.* hallucination.

delusional (paranoid) disorder formerly called paranoia, a mental disorder characterized by delusions (q.v.), especially of jealousy, grandeur, or persecution, but with otherwise unimpaired intellectual functioning.

dendrite from the Greek *dendron*, tree, the collection of branched, threadlike extensions of a neuron (q.v.) that receives impulses from other neurons or from a receptor and conducts them towards the cell body.

deoxyribonucleic acid (DNA) a self-replicating molecule, the major constituent of chromosomes (q.v.), containing the hereditary information transmitted from parents to offspring in all organisms apart from some viruses (including the AIDS virus), and consisting of two strands coiled into a double helix linked by hydrogen bonds between the complementary chemical bases that encode the genetic information – between adenine and thymine and between cytosine and guanine. *See also* gene.

depression a sustained negative mood state characterized by sadness, pessimism, a general feeling of despondency, passivity, indecisiveness, suicidal thoughts, sleep disturbances, and other mental and physical symptoms, associated with some mood disorders (q.v.).

diazepam one of the benzodiazepine drugs (q.v.), commonly called Valium.

dissociative disorder an umbrella term for psychological disorders, such as multiple personality disorder (q.v.) and the non-organic amnesias, involving dissociation and general disintegration of the functions of consciousness, self-concept, or perceptual-motor coordination.

dizygotic (fraternal) twins from the Greek *dis*, double, + zygote, a fertilized egg cell, from the Greek *zygon*, yoke, non-identical twins arising from the fertilization of two separate eggs by two separate sperms at about the same time, who like ordinary siblings share half their genes in common. *Cf.* monozygotic (identical) twins.

DNA *see* deoxyribonucleic acid (DNA).

dominant gene a gene (q.v.) inherited from one parent that produces the same phenotype (q.v.) in the organism whether the corresponding allele (q.v.) inherited from the other parent is the same or different. *Cf.* recessive gene. *See also* epistasis.

dopamine a catecholamine (q.v.); one of the neurotransmitter (q.v.) substances significantly involved in central nervous system (q.v.) functioning. *See also* antidepressant drugs.

double-blind study a research design in which, in order to control for experimenter effects and the effects of demand characteristics, neither the experimenter nor the subjects know, until after the data have been collected, which experimental treatment has been applied to which subjects. This type of design is used, for example, in drug trials, with the help of placebos (q.v.), to avoid contamination of the results from biases and preconceptions on the part of the experimenter or the subjects.

efferent neurons from the Latin *e*, from, *ferre*, to carry, neurons that transmit impulses away from the central nervous system (CNS) towards the muscles, glands, etc. *Cf.* afferent neurons.

electrodermal response (EDR) *see* galvanic skin response (GSR).

electroencephalogram (EEG) from the Greek *electron*, amber (in which electricity was first observed), *en*, in, *kephale*, head, *gramme*, line, a visual record of the electrical activity of the brain, recorded via electrodes attached to the scalp. The recording apparatus is called an electroencephalograph. *See also* alpha waves, delta waves.

endocrine gland any ductless gland, such as the adrenal gland or pituitary gland (qq.v.), that secretes hormones directly into the bloodstream. The endocrine system functions as an elaborate signalling system within the body, alongside the nervous system.

endorphins from the Greek *endon*, within, and morphine, from *Morpheus*, the Greek god of sleep and dreams, any of a class of morphine-like substances occurring naturally in the brain that bind to pain receptors and thus block pain sensations.

epinephrine, norepinephrine from the Greek *epi*, upon, *nephros*, kidney, alternative words for adrenalin and noradrenalin (qq.v.), especially in United States usage. *See also* endocrine gland.

epistasis from the Greek word meaning stoppage, in genetics, the suppression by a gene of the effect of another gene that is not its allele. *Cf.* dominant gene.

ESS *see* evolutionarily stable strategy (ESS).

ethology from the Greek *ethos*, character, *logos*, study, the study of the behaviour of animals in their natural habitats.

evoked potential a characteristic pattern in an electroencephalogram (EEG) in response to a specific stimulus.

evolutionarily stable strategy (ESS) in behaviour genetics and behavioural ecology, any genetically determined pattern of behaviour that is stable in the sense that it would be favoured by natural selection (q.v.) in competition with alternative behaviour patterns. The word 'strategy' in this context comes from game theory (q.v.).

family study *see* consanguinity study.

5-hydroxytryptamine (5-HT) another name for serotonin (q.v.).

fluoxetine hydrochloride *see under* antidepressant drugs.

fraternal twins *see* dizygotic (fraternal) twins.

galvanic skin response (GSR) a fall in the resistance of the skin to the passage of a weak electric current, indicative of emotion or arousal, also called psychogalvanic response (PGR) and electrodermal response (EDR).

game theory a branch of mathematics, with applications in social psychology, behavioural ecology, and sociobiology, devoted to the analysis of interdependent decision-making in any situation in which two or more decision makers, called players, each choose between two or more options, called strategies, and the outcome depends on the choices of all players. *See also* evolutionarily stable strategy (ESS).

gene from the Greek *genes*, born, the unit of hereditary transmission encoded in deoxyribonucleic acid (DNA) (q.v.), occupying a fixed locus on a chromosome (q.v.), and either specifying the formation of a protein or part of a protein (structural gene) or regulating or repressing the operation of other genes (operator or repressor gene). The complete human genome contains between 50,000 and 100,000 genes. *See also* allele, dominant gene, epistasis, recessive gene.

genotype the complete genetic constitution of an organism. *See also* gene.

glial cells cells forming the connecting tissue that surrounds and supports neurons (q.v.) in the nervous system.

GSR *see* galvanic skin response (GSR).

hallucination from the Latin *alucinari*, to wander in the mind, a false perception, most commonly visual or auditory, subjectively similar or identical to an ordinary perception but occurring in the absence of relevant sensory stimuli, characteristic in particular of some forms of schizophrenia. False perceptions occurring during sleep, while falling asleep (hypnagogic image), or while awakening (hypnopompic image) are not normally considered to be hallucinations. *Cf.* delusion.

hallucinogenic drugs drugs such as lysergic acid diethylamide (LSD) or mescaline that induce hallucinations.

heritability the proportion of variance in a phenotypic trait that is attributable to genetic variance in a specified population.

hippocampus from the Greek *hippos*, horse, *kampos*, sea monster, a structure in the brain, whose cross section has the shape of a sea horse, involved in emotion, motivation, learning, and the establishment of long-term memory.

homeostasis from the Greek *homos*, same, *stasis*, stoppage, the maintenance of equilibrium in any physiological or psychological process by automatic compensation for disrupting changes.

hormone from the Greek *horman*, to stir up or urge on, a chemical substance secreted into the bloodstream by an endocrine gland (q.v.) and transported to another part of the body where it exerts a specific effect.

hypnotics barbiturates and benzodiazepine drugs (qq.v.) used as sleeping drugs to treat insomnia (q.v.) and known informally as sleeping drugs.

hypothalamus a pea-sized structure situated (as its name indicates) below the thalamus at the base of the brain, crucially involved in the regulation of the autonomic nervous system (q.v.) and the control of temperature, heart-rate, blood pressure, hunger, thirst, and sexual arousal.

imipramine *see under* antidepressant drugs.

imprinting in ethology (q.v.), a form of rapid learning that takes place during a critical period (q.v.) of development and is extremely resistant to extinction. The most familiar example is the behaviour of newly hatched ducklings, which will become imprinted on, and subsequently follow around, virtually any moving object that is presented during this critical period.

insomnia difficulty in falling or remaining asleep. Initial insomnia is difficulty in falling asleep; middle insomnia is waking up and going back to sleep only with difficulty; and terminal insomnia (which is less lethal than other terminal disorders) is waking up at least two hours before one's normal waking time and being unable to fall asleep again. *See also* hypnotics.

ions atoms or groups of atoms that have either lost one or more electrons and therefore carry positive electrical charges (cations, q.v.) or gained one or more electrons and therefore carry negative electrical charges (anions, q.v.).

kinship study *see* consanguinity study.

Largactil the trademark of a preparation of one of the antipsychotic drugs (q.v.), chlorpromazine.

LD-50 the dosage of any drug that is lethal to 50 per cent of subjects. *Cf.* minimum effective dose (MED-50). *See also* therapeutic index.

Librium the trademark of a preparation of the drug chlordiazepoxide (q.v.). *See also* benzodiazepine drugs.

limbic system a ring of structures surrounding the brain stem concerned with emotion, hunger, and sex.

linkage in genetics, the occurrence of two genes (q.v.) close together on the same chromosome (q.v.) so that they are unlikely to become separated and tend to be inherited together.

lithium *see under* antipsychotic drugs.

longitudinal study a research design in which the same sample of subjects (q.v.) is examined repeatedly over an extended span of time, typically to investigate problems of developmental psychology.

magnetic resonance imaging (MRI) a non-invasive method of examining the brain or other body organs by recording the responses of atoms, molecules, or nuclei in a magnetic field to radio waves or other forms of energy. *Cf.* CT (computerized tomography), PET (positron emission tomography).

major tranquillizers *see under* antipsychotic drugs.

mania a mood disorder characterized by extreme elation, expansiveness, irritability, talkativeness, inflated self-esteem, and flight of ideas.

manic-depressive psychosis *see* bipolar disorder.

MAO inhibitor *see under* antidepressant drugs.

medulla short for medulla oblongata, the lower stalklike part of the brain stem, attached to the spinal cord, involved in vegetative processes such as heartbeat and breathing.

mental disorder according to the *Diagnostic and Statistical Manual of Mental Disorders* of the American Psychiatric Association (DSM-IV), a psychological or behavioural syndrome or pattern associated with distress (a painful symptom), disability (impairment in one or more areas of functioning), and a significantly increased risk of death, pain, disability, or an important loss of freedom, occurring not merely as a predictable response to a disturbing life-event.

minimum effective dose (MED-50) the lowest dosage of a drug required to produce the desired effect in 50 per cent of subjects. *Cf.* LD-50. *See also* therapeutic index.

minor tranquillizers another name for anti-anxiety drugs (q.v.).

monoamine oxidase inhibitor (MAOI) *see under* antidepressant drugs.

monozygotic (identical) twins from the Greek *monos*, single, + zygote, a fertilized egg cell, from the Greek *zygon*, yoke, twins who are formed when a single egg is fertilized by a single sperm and then splits into two. Unlike the more common dizygotic (fraternal) twins, monozygotic (identical) twins share identical genes.

mood disorders a group of mental disorders (q.v.) characterized by disturbances of affect or mood, including especially depression, bipolar disorder and mania (qq.v.).

multiple personality disorder a rare dissociative disorder (q.v.) in which two or more markedly different personalities coexist within the same individual, popularly confused with schizophrenia (q.v.).

natural selection the evolutionary process whereby those individuals from a population that are best adapted to the environment survive and produce more offspring than others, thus altering the composition of the population and eventually the characteristics of the species as a whole.

nervous system *see under* autonomic nervous system, central nervous system (CNS), parasympathetic nervous system, sympathetic nervous system.

neuron from the Greek word for nerve, a nerve cell, which is the basic structural and functional unit of the nervous system, consisting of a cell body, axon, and dendrites (qq.v.). *See also* afferent neuron, efferent neuron.

neurophysiology the study of the operation of the nervous system (q.v.).

neuroscience an interdisciplinary field of study concerned with the anatomy, physiology, development, and biochemistry of the nervous system (q.v.), and its effects on behaviour and mental experience.

neurotransmitter a chemical substance such as acetylcholine, dopamine, serotonin, or noradrenalin (qq.v.) by which a neuron (q.v.) communicates with another neuron or with a muscle or gland.

noradrenalin one of the catecholamine (q.v.) hormones (q.v.) and an important neurotransmitter (q.v.) in the nervous system (q.v.), also called norepinephrine, especially in United States usage.

norepinephrine *see* noradrenalin.

normal distribution a symmetrical, bell-shaped probability distribution, with the most probable scores concentrated around the mean (average) and progressively less probable scores occurring further from the mean: 68.26 per cent of scores fall within one standard deviation (q.v.) on either side of the mean, 95.44 per cent fall within two standard deviations, and 99.75 fall within three standard deviations. Because of the central limit theorem (q.v.), the normal distribution approximates the observed frequency distributions of many psychological and biological variables and is widely used in inferential statistics.

obsessions recurrent, persistent, irrational ideas, thoughts, images, or impulses that are experienced not as voluntary but as unwanted invasions of consciousness, characteristic especially of obsessive-compulsive disorder (q.v.).

obsessive-compulsive disorder one of the more common anxiety disorders characterized, as the name suggests, by obsessions and compulsions (qq.v.)

panic disorder an anxiety disorder characterized by panic attacks, overwhelming apprehension, dread or terror, fear of going insane or dying, and fight or flight behaviour.

paranoia *see* delusional (paranoid) disorder.

parasympathetic nervous system one of the two major divisions of the autonomic nervous system; its general function is to conserve metabolic energy. *Cf.* sympathetic nervous system.

peptides chemical substances such as endorphins (q.v.) that regulate various bodily functions and play an important part in the experience of pain.

PET (positron emission tomography) a non-invasive technique for scanning the brain and studying its function by recording the emission of positrons when radioactive glucose, introduced into the brain, is metabolized by neurons (q.v.) as they are activated. Tomography, from the Greek *tome*, a cutting, is any of a number of techniques used to obtain images of selected plane sections of the human body or other solid objects. *Cf.* CT (computerized tomography), magnetic resonance imaging (MRI).

phenotype the physical and psychological characteristics of an organism, determined jointly by its genetic constitution and its environment.

pheromone from the Greek *pherein*, to bear, *horman*, to stimulate, any chemical substance with a communicative function, secreted externally by an organism and affecting the behaviour or physiology of other members of the same species.

phobia from the Greek *phobos*, fear, an irrational, debilitating, persistent, and intense fear of a specific type of object, activity, or situation, which, if certain diagnostic criteria are fulfilled, may be considered a mental disorder (q.v.).

pituitary gland the master endocrine gland (q.v.), attached by a stalk to the base of the brain, which secretes into the bloodstream hormones affecting bodily growth and the functioning of other endocrine glands.

placebo from the Latin word meaning I shall please (the opening words of the Roman Catholic office or service for the dead are *Placebo Domino*, I shall please the Lord), an inactive substance or dummy treatment administered to a control group to compare its effects with those of a real drug or treatment. *See also* double-blind study, placebo effect.

placebo effect a positive or therapeutic benefit resulting from the administration of a placebo (q.v.) to someone who believes that the treatment is real.

pons from the Latin word meaning bridge, short for pons Varolii (bridge of Varoli, after the Italian anatomist Costanzo Varoli), a rounded structure connecting the two halves of the brain at the level of the brain stem.

positron emission tomography *see* PET (positron emission tomography).

process in anatomy, an axon or a dendrite extending from a neuron (qq.v.).

Prozac the proprietary name for fluoxetine hydrochloride, one of the antidepressant drugs (q.v.).

psychoactive drug any drug such as lysergic acid diethylamide (LSD), opium, or a barbiturate, that is capable of affecting mental activity. *See also* amphetamine, anti-anxiety drugs, antidepressant drugs, antipsychotic drugs, barbiturates, benzodiazepine drugs, hallucinogenic drugs, psychopharmacology.

psychogalvanic response (PGR) *see* galvanic skin response (GSR).

psychoneuroimmunology the study of the interrelationships between mental function, the nervous system (q.v.), and the immune system.

psychopharmacology the study of drugs that have psychological effects. *See also* amphetamine, anti-anxiety drugs, antidepressant drugs, antipsychotic drugs, barbiturates, benzodiazepine drugs, hallucinogenic drugs, LD-50, minimum effective dose (MED-50), psychoactive drugs, therapeutic index.

psychosis gross impairment of psychological functioning, including loss of self-insight and of contact with reality, such as is found in mental disorders involving hallucinations and delusions (qq.v.).

rapid eye movement (REM) rapid movement of the eyeballs behind closed eyelids during sleep, when the sleeper is in REM sleep, a state that occurs approximately every 90 minutes when sleeping and is characterized by vivid dreaming. *See also* REM rebound effect.

receptor a sense organ or structure that is sensitive to a specific form of physical energy and that transmits neural information to other parts of the nervous system (q.v.).

recessive gene a gene (q.v.) inherited from one parent that produces its characteristic phenotype (q.v.) in an organism only when the corresponding gene inherited from the other parent is the same. *Cf.* dominant gene.

reciprocal altruism altruism (q.v.) or helping behaviour whose performance or continuation is conditional on the recipient behaving altruistically or helpfully in return.

recombinant DNA techniques techniques involving the joining together by chemical means of DNA (q.v.) molecules extracted from different sources, for example when DNA from a human gene is recombined with DNA from a bacterium in order to create a new genetic form.

REM rebound effect the tendency for people who are deprived of REM sleep to show increased proportions of REM sleep on subsequent nights.

REM sleep *see under* rapid eye movement (REM).

reticular activating system (RAS) a large bundle of neurons (q.v.) in the brain stem responsible, as its name suggests, for controlling the level of arousal or activation of the cerebral cortex (q.v.), and generally involved in consciousness, sleep, and muscular tone.

schizophrenia from the Greek *schizein*, to split, *phren*, mind, a group of mental disorders characterized by incoherent thought and speech, hallucinations (q.v.), delusions (q.v.), flattened or inappropriate affect, deterioration of social functioning, and lack of self-care. In spite of its derivation, the word does not refer to multiple personality disorder (q.v.).

serotonin one of the neurotransmitter (q.v.) substances in the nervous system, also known as 5-hydroxytryptamine or 5-HT.

slow-wave sleep deep, dreamless sleep, characterized by high-amplitude (150 microvolts), low-frequency (1–3 Hz) electroencephalogram (EEG) waves called delta waves (q.v.).

sociobiology the study of the biological bases of social behaviour.

soma *see* cell body.

stimulants hormones such as adrenalin, noradrenalin, and dopamine (qq.v.), and drugs such as amphetamines (q.v.), that increase physiological arousal in general and central nervous system (q.v.) activity in particular.

sympathetic nervous system one of the two major divisions of the autonomic nervous system (q.v.); it is concerned with general activation, and it mobilizes the body's reaction to stress or perceived danger. *Cf.* parasympathetic nervous system.

synapse the junction between two neurons (q.v.), where nerve impulses are relayed from the axon (q.v.) of one neuron to the dendrites (q.v.) of another.

thalamus from the Greek *thalamos*, an inner room or bedroom, a major interior brain structure that serves as a relay centre to the cerebral cortex (q.v.) for all sensory impulses except those arising from olfaction.

therapeutic index the ratio obtained by dividing the LD-50 of a drug by its minimum effective dose (MED-50): mathematically, the therapeutic index $TI = (LD\text{-}50)/(MED\text{-}50)$. If the ratio is equal to 10 or more, it indicates that a lethal dose is at least ten times the minimum effective dose. *See also* LD-50, minimum effective dose (MED-50).

tranquillizers *see under* anti-anxiety drugs, antipsychotic drugs.

tricyclic antidepressants *see* antidepressant drugs.

Valium a trademark of a preparation of the drug diazepam (q.v.). *See also* benzodiazepine drugs.

zygote from the Greek *zygon*, yoke, a fertilized ovum or egg.

INDEX

acetylcholine 99–100
activated sleep 72
adaptation 29, 31–4
addiction xiii, 105–6
adoption studies 5
  Colorado adoption project 10
  and IQ 6, 7, 10
  and schizophrenia 11–12
altruism xi, 38–40
amygdala 58, 59
animal behaviour genetics x, 1–2,
    13–24
animals, sleep 69
anti-anxiety drugs xiii, 94, 95, 107–8
antidepressant drugs xiii, 94, 95, 108–9
antipsychotic drugs xiii, 94, 95, 106–7
anxiety, drug treatments xiii, 94, 95,
    107–8
Aplysia, egg laying behaviour 21–4
Aserinsky, E. xii, 76
auditory system *see* hearing
autonomic nervous system (ANS) 52–3
  chemical transmission 99–100
Axel, R. 22
Axelrod, R. 38
axons 48, 50

barbiturates 107
basal ganglia 58
Bastock, M. 2
behaviour
  effect of single genes on 15
  functions of sleep 81
  mechanisms of drug actions 103–9
  role of genetics and environment x,
    2, 102–3
behavioural ecology
  methods and prospects 44
  scope of 35–44

theory x–xi, 29–35
behavioural genetics
  animal 13–24
  history of 1–2
  human x, 6–12
  research methods 4–5, 8–10
behavioural tolerance 105–6
Bell, C. 54
Benzer, S. 15, 16
Bernard, C. 98
biological rhythms 16–19
bipolar disorder x, xiii, 12, 108
Bodmer, W.F. x
Bouchard, T.J. 6
brain xi–xii
  cerebral cortex 60–6
  divisions 52, 54
    hindbrain structures 54–6
    midbrain structures 56–7
    forebrain structures 57–60
  link with environment and behaviour
    102–3
  mechanisms of drug action 95,
    98–103
Broadhurst, P.L. 2
Broca, P. 58
Brodmann, K. 63–4
Burt, C. 6

cells
  glial 47–8
  pyramidal 62–3
  stellate cells 63
  see also neurons
central nervous system 52
  effect of drugs on 103–4
cerebellum 55–6
cerebral cortex
  architectonic maps of 63–5